THE IMPRACTICAL CABINETMAKER

THE IMPRACTICAL CABINETMAKER

JAMES KRENOV

VNR VAN NOSTRAND REINHOLD COMPANY
New York   Cincinnati   Toronto   London   Melbourne

Acknowledgment

This book is an attempt to share a few questions (and experiences). Some of the questions proved to be near at hand, others came from people far away who were—and are—sincerely concerned about our craft and how they hope to live with it in a way that leaves them happy.

Books like these, it is said, take a bit of doing. One does need friends. I came to New York City (and Van Nostrand Reinhold) with an overload of pages and photographs. Out of this heap there emerged, with the truly sensitive help of my editor Barbara Kelman-Burgower, a semblance of order. As on previous occasions, Nancy N. Green kept an understanding eye on things, while Louis Vasquez did the important artwork that is all too apt to be taken for granted.

James Krenov

Also by James Krenov
A Cabinetmaker's Notebook (1975)
The Fine Art of Cabinetmaking (1976)

Copyright © 1979 by Litton Educational Publishing, Inc.
Library of Congress Catalog Card Number 79-943
ISBN 0-442-24558-0

Printed in the United States of America
Designed by Loudan Enterprises
Photographs by the author and Bengt Carlén

Published in 1979 by Van Nostrand Reinhold Company
A division of Litton Educational Publishing, Inc.
135 West 50th Street, New York, NY 10020, U.S.A.

Van Nostrand Reinhold Limited
1410 Birchmount Road
Scarborough, Ontario M1P 2E7, Canada

Van Nostrand Reinhold Australia Pty. Ltd.
17 Queen Street
Mitcham, Victoria 3132, Australia

Van Nostrand Reinhold Company Limited
Molly Millars Lane
Wokingham, Berkshire, England

16 15 14 13 12 11 10 9 8 7 6 5 4 3 2 1

Library of Congress Cataloging in Publication Data

Krenov, James.
    The impractical cabinetmaker.

    Includes index.
    1. Cabinet-work.   I. Title.
TT197.K69   684.1   79-943
ISBN 0-442-24558-0

FRONTISPIECE: *Detail of Italian walnut writing table.*

Different people, different ways. . . .
D. H. Lawrence

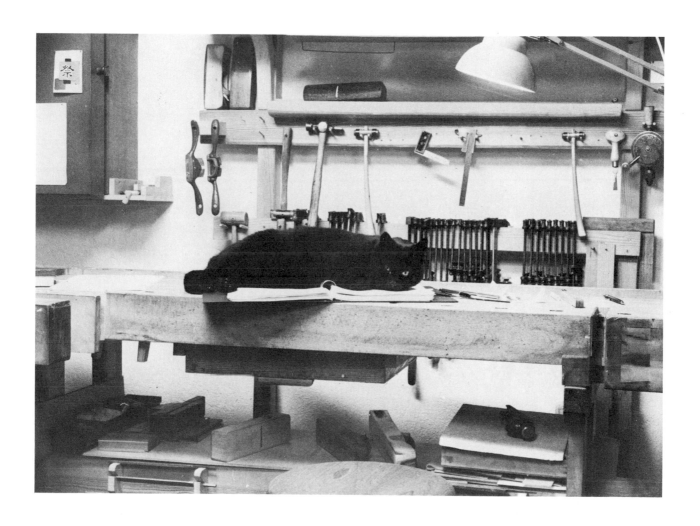

Today people are going into crafts for reasons other than those of ten or twenty years ago. True, some of those reasons are still valid. But now they are spiced with emotion. There is more emotion in doing crafts now than there has been for a long, long time. And emotion in the way we regard crafts, as well. We used to judge crafts on the basis of tradition, a sense of quality some of us grew up with, a certain everyday knowledge of crafts methods. The public approach was generally one of understanding and calm appraisal. Now, however, curiosity is increasingly replacing knowledge—often with dubious results for both craftsman and public. Nowadays people are attracted to craftwork emotionally, more because they *want* it than because they *need* it. Like the good news/bad news joke, there are two sides to this situation. The good is that more people are getting involved; the bad is that the result is often less pleasing than it ought to be. But it's possible to change this: If responsible people help the emotion along with relevant evaluation, it will be an asset to us all. If not, we are headed for trouble.

Contents

Woodcraft Today

Woodworking, or woodcraft, has undergone a number of very great changes during the last ten or fifteen years. These changes are not only in the ways of work—the modernization of methods even in what we call the handcrafted object—but also in the differing attitudes of individual woodworkers toward the work itself and in the relationship of the craftsman to his fellows in society. Two hundred and more years ago artisans worked at making utilitarian objects in wood and they were filling a very real need: producing useful everyday things in wood, whether they were furniture or wooden utensils or tools. Then came the industrial revolution, and with it the mechanization or, at best, effectivization of woodworking and cabinetmaking as such. On the edge of this we have now a new version of the artisan, the cabinetmaker or woodworker producing even less than did his preindustrial counterpart and doing so in a different way. There are now few craftsmen engaged in making fine furniture on a scale that will satisfy an extensive need. As matters stand today, there really is not a *need* for handcrafted furniture—at least not as furniture. On the other hand, people are becoming newly aware of and attracted by unique, crafted objects of wood as a contrast to the industrially produced counterpart, as a one-of-a-kind expression of the craftsman's personal message. Result: a small nucleus of craftsmen who not only survive by their work, but even prosper. These craftsmen are individualists in the marketable sense; they tend to express their own ambitions, techniques, and concepts of form—one might say their image—in the furniture or other things they make of wood. This is a new role for the craftsman, or at least a new definition. He is both craftsman and artist, although not necessarily in that order. In fact, many craftsmen are able to do well by being artists first and craftsmen second. To do so they must above all be imaginative in their work, which often means being eccentric. Some establish, others follow, trends of eccentricity or avant-garde expression. They are realistically competitive in marketing their things, or having them presented by others. They are in touch with what is happening in craft and in art. They're "with it."

That is the glossy side of craft today: the new, visibly successful artisan-craftsman who sets the pace in the light of standards that are those of the current idiom, approved by people writing about crafts and art, but which are not necessarily craftsmen's standards in the sense of lasting values and integrity. In this conspicuous area of crafts there is a great deal of competition and a disturbing amount of catering to public taste and trends, even if it means—as it so often does—giving up one's personal standards to satisfy a market demand. It is a very pressured existence into which most of the really successful craftsmen are forced.

Some of us see a danger in this kind of success. At the same time as a few self-assured craftsmen set a style and draw attention to the media in which they work, they are creating norms and standards that often are a handicap to others who, perhaps by their nature and methods, are less competitive. The emergence of superstar craftsmen is but one strand of development in woodcraft today; a second, and I think more important, tendency is that a great number of people (one could say *craftsmen*, but I prefer to say just people), mostly young, are working with wood on a nonprofessional basis. They are not established, nor are they "successful"—many of them do not aspire to be successful in the ordinary meaning of the word. These are all sorts of people, and they are working with wood for varied reasons: for fun, for therapy, to make things they need at home, for their children, or for friends. And, certainly, they often do it out of sheer curiosity. They probably have one common bond: They are seeking enjoyment and satisfaction in working with wood in a modest, somewhat apologetic way. (The reasons for the apologetic attitude will be gone into later on.) Some have had a bit of schooling, whether in manual training or in college woodworking, and it has left them not entirely satisfied. They may have found out something about the working of the craft as a profession, but even toward the end of their studies they did not know enough about themselves and what in all this professional information and craft talk was usable for them. Along with a certain amount of know-how they have accumulated a great number of questions as to what they are going to do with their acquired knowledge, how they can relate it to their way of living.

Even more of these people have had no craft education at all. They've simply come across wood for one reason or another, found it interesting, and have begun to putter with it, or they have seen others puttering with it, and this has attracted them. This represents a very large and still growing group of woodworkers, young and old. Some are involved in other professions and are simply hobby-minded and wood-interested. They can be mechanics or executives or whatever. They constitute a positive phenomenon, not only a craft phenomenon but a social one as well. I don't think we quite understand the inner workings of this group, much less its real mood.

Here is a new and puzzling aspect of crafts. The basic change in the last, let us say, ten years is that a large part of craftwork has evolved from being a profession—that is, a way of *making* a living—to *being* a way of living. More and more people are taking up crafts because they feel a need for intimate contact with a material; it provides certain inner satisfactions. Structured goal-oriented education doesn't quite fit these people. Neither does all the professional information that they are being fed—the dos and don'ts and hairsplitting discussions and letters-to-the-editor. There is information and knowledge there, certainly, and much of it is usable; but the way it is presented lacks flexibility. It lacks the warmth and appeal these people need. It does not help them to a personal approach, an alternative to the purely efficient method that is so prevalent. No wonder the craftsmen who consider themselves "professionals," or who write for magazines, or teach, are prone to look upon these outsiders—these amateurs or enthusiasts—as being impractical.

We tend to measure an outsider by looking down. So these people, whether they have a proper answer or not, whether they are sure of themselves in what they want to do or are merely groping, are embarrassed and somewhat apologetic when approached by those with more knowledge and more professional experience. Even the common ground of craft has its pitfalls.

I suppose there are basically two different types of craftsmen: those who are practical and those who are not. The first type is a very realistic, efficiency-minded, survival-oriented person for whom getting things done is primary. "You are not a good craftsman if you cannot live by your work," they say. I believe this statement to be not only historically untrue, but also unnecessarily cruel. Seeing craft as a livelihood (business, really) does make sense to many; it always will. But that's only one type of person.

The other type is less easy to define. I hope that what I mean will gradually emerge in the course of this book. But for now, and for want of a better expression, I am talking about the impractical but dedicated amateur. He can be seen as the opposite of the first type. He is the craftsman for whom an atmosphere of much-to-sell is a hindrance to doing his best always—and living accordingly. He is an idealist who wants to survive to have the chance to work with wood, but not at the price of having woodworking become something less than he hoped it would be.

To each his choice. It is likely that this state of affairs will result in a parting of the ways; already there are signs of estrangement between business-oriented (that is, trend- and market-oriented) craftsmen and those otherwise inclined.

Yes, there is a split, and not neatly down the middle either. Maybe it's the realists versus the dreamers now, the organized this-is-the-way-you-do-it, you've-got-to-make-a-living people opposed to the dreamers who say, "You don't have to 'do it,' or necessarily do all that much of it, unless you enjoy the doing." Enjoyment is uppermost for them. Some of us may not agree. We may even pretend that these "enjoyers" are unimportant, or that they are very quaint and out of step, but that they will learn the realities of life soon enough. . . . Still, we can't quite ignore them because they are many. And they are here to stay.

To those who say one has to learn how to do it the professional way, the widely accepted way, these naive and curious people say, "Maybe, but I've got all my life to learn *that*. Right now I want to know what my own way of doing things should be. I want to find what is right for *me*. And when I find it, whatever it is, whatever way of working it means, then I will go about ac-

quiring some more knowledge and maybe some mechanical equipment, and other things I need. But if I start at the usual this-is-how-to-make-and-sell end, I might get bogged down there and never reach the point where I'm asking the right questions. I'm willing to learn. But I want to learn what I need so I can work—and like it. Who wants to be unhappy as a craftsman? All these people are telling me I don't know what I need; I should learn it all and then sort it out, they say. I can't digest that much. I want to learn what is important and interesting to me now. From there on, I'll take my chances. . . ."

The order of things, the way these woodworkers go about learning, is as strange to some of us as the way they work. Or what they want to express in their work, which is their philosophy of living.

This situation, with so many craftsmen in wood working modestly, nonprofessionally, searching for both enjoyment and intrinsic values, is a reflection of more than a crafts mood. It is also a rebellion against rigidity and the established measures of success in craft. It's a positive force because, for the first time, people are emerging who seriously want to express themselves spontaneously and simply, not necessarily to a wide audience, but as a form of individual adventure and satisfaction. They try to find a way of living that allows them to do this without being pressured, or ridiculed, to win a few friends, gain a small but warm audience, maybe one day make a bare living by their craft. In all this there is an implied questioning of the sort of education and certain trends that have become more or less the rule in craft. I do not think that educators have realized the full significance of this; certainly others in responsible positions in the world of craft misunderstand some of it. Although it is true that many organizations and associations are honestly engaged in helping craftsmen, distributing information, reviewing shows, and so on, it is also true that the people in a craft, in this case woodworking, who get the most attention are those who have already succeeded.

Many of us want to know not only what is being done here and there, but also how it relates to certain aesthetics and sensitivity, what some regard as fixed points in our craft universe. There are, and should be, measures by which we can honestly get our bearings. Some of us who write about crafts are not pausing to include these points of orientation along with our reportage, human interest stories, and awed attention to the eccentric aspect of woodworking. We are not doing enough for those who would excel anonymously or merely within a small circle. We don't seem to know where these people are and what they need in the way of help and encouragement. Ordinary professional or craft information is only a part of what they need. The rest of it is as yet rather vague but it consists of aesthetics, the integrity of the material weighed against various methods—judged, not with hair-splitting exactness, but in relation to skill, intuition, and reverence for the life that is in wood. There is too little constructive evaluation. After the artiness has been aired, the exposition of clearcut rights and wrongs terminated, we should still have a lot to talk about, and share.

It has never been my belief that experience or professional knowledge is anyone's personal property. It has never occurred to me that if someone comes and asks me this or that, or wants to know how to do something or why one does it in a certain way, that I would not take the time to answer the question, if I can. Or that I should say, "Well, it took me twenty years to learn, and I'm not going to give it away for free." This simply is not the way I look at experience or knowledge. I've picked up a bit of know-how, yes. Most of it has been used by craftsmen long before me. It is not my private knowledge, but rather it is my way of using what little I have learned that happens to be right for people like myself. It pleases me tremendously to know there are others who look at it likewise. Some of us craftsmen have periods of doubt and fear, and getting a bit of help, sharing information and feelings with other people can, at those times, make the difference between getting on with one's

work with enjoyment or slipping into discouragement and confusion, which can end in resignation.

I'd like to believe that between one kind of craftsman and another, between the realist and the dreamer, the successful person and the unknown enthusiast, there is a mutual understanding. But I'm not so sure. Society being what it is and the demands it makes upon us force us into rigid patterns; even the new, "relaxed," folksy crafts are pressed into a monotony of sorts. All the same, I continue to hope that the communication between the two types will be generous and tolerant. For the time being, however, there are irritations; too much attention is paid to some trends and not enough to others. I'm inclined to believe that even in the long run there will be certain irreconcilable differences between craftsmen, just as there are between people in general. "Different people, different ways." All we can hope for, then, is that different people will find their happiness in different ways and will be allowed to continue along the path they have chosen, the one that is right for them.

Not long ago I was asked: "What does the word *work* mean to you?" After some hesitation I said, "I guess it means doing what one thinks is worth doing, and doing it well." Our conversation circled around that *well*; it seems to me even now a key word. For one craftsman it means getting the work done by the most efficient means at hand. His satisfaction is the result, the piece. And that piece is for him—as it is for the intended audience—primarily a visual experience. *How* it was achieved is less important than *what* it is. Although if ingenuity had a part in the process, so much the better; with it one feels the nearness of originality. We are asked to look at the outcome. Look indeed. Any one of us will claim to have looked, but what we saw differs: The result means different things to different people, depending on what one looks for, which, in turn, reflects what is important to each of us.

It occurs to me here that one can hardly define any criteria in a craft without relating it

to the ability to perceive what is important. And with that word, *important*, as with *well*, we are at a point of division: For what has long been the bulk of our crafts public the immediate visual message is enough, provided it pleases the eye. Crafts attention, especially in America and England, has come to center on originality of expression; consequently, there is a tendency to hasty judgment, an approach that is dangerously superficial. This is saddening. Besides being stubborn and illusive, wood is a noble material. Part of a craftsman's purpose in life should be to establish a living relationship with his material and its innate qualities. This is difficult to do when those who promote and judge woodcrafts keep repeating words like *form*, *originality*, *design*; the echoes are bound to affect educators as well as craftsmen. The result is a simplification, a crudeness in some of the ways we are taught. All too often we are prone to use quick, purely visual effects as a means to bypass skill and dedication. If you can't make it good, make it weird. Such shortcuts are applauded. Responsible—or is it merely influential?—people urge woodworkers toward an expression ever more similar to that of some far-out pottery. We get things that remind us of melting chocolate, something from a bakery, gooey objects in wood, bad imitations of art nouveau. At the other extreme we have a touch of the mechanical in the finished pieces themselves; with their perfect circles (or radii of these) and sharp edges, they resemble machine parts turned to wood.

There is a contradiction, a sense of absurdity in such a situation: *The craftsman wants to make a personal statement, but he uses efficiency-motivated, impersonal methods to achieve it.* To an increasing number of us it simply does not make sense. Handmade, yes. The logical question is: "Whose

hands?" That is the crucial question. Originality becomes a compulsion when the way we work denies us a sense of closeness to our material, a sense of participation in a process that should give an inner satisfaction and also lend still another dimension to what we have done. It is a mystery to me why this is not more apparent. Probably one of the main reasons is an all-too-competitive craft environment.

Lately, however, there are signs of a tendency away from this visually motivated, result-is-all attitude. In at least some quarters, a fundamental change is taking

Wall cabinet, Italian walnut. Height about 83cm, width 41cm. Surfaces hand-planed; wax finish outside, polish inside. 1978. Doors here are a bookmatch resulting in a soft, almost three-dimensional curve. An opposite matching would give a hard-cornered feeling.

place with regard to the meaning of work itself. At a time when to many of us life is so strangely complex with its problems of identity and fulfillment, work takes on new meaning: To do something we enjoy is to begin to know ourselves. Philosophical talk and all kinds of uneasy moving around won't by themselves give us wholeness. We need to work in a way that is satisfying. How lucky are we who have the chance to do this in a generous way! Oh, the result of our work is still important—only a fool would deny that—but the emphasis has changed. For a certain kind of person that means doing more than just a piece with something visual going for it. This craftsman wants to approach the work itself as having a definite and vital connection between the *methods* to be used and the *nature* of the result. It is not merely the originality of its design, nor signs of technical dexterity, but the very nature of the piece that concerns him. He experiences what's *in* it, the sum total of what he has put into the process from beginning to end, from the first attitude and idea, through each little step and experience —all of it. And that, finally, is the piece: the message of satisfying work skillfully done. An intimacy. This craftsman, too, says, "There it is, look," though now he is apt to add, ". . . closely, please."

It seems that more and more people planning to go into a craft are looking not so much for a school as for a teacher. And this signals a change in attitude about learning. The student feels that along with certain basic skills, he needs to learn something about himself. In order to do that, he needs help from someone who really cares about him *as a person*. This need for more personalized education is a significant change; I think it will result in an increased interest in those schools that offer flexibility and a close relationship between teacher and student. A college dean making a farewell speech not long ago voiced the opinion that perhaps the very large, prestigious institutions offering long, structured programs have seen their day. The trend in the next few years may well be toward smaller schools, special courses, and more personal attitudes on the part of both schools and educators. Some rather basic suppositions are being challenged, among them the one that schools know more about what crafts students need—and want—to learn than do the students themselves. Three years and $20,000 is an awful lot to pay. . . . Schools offering excellence or distinguished reputations should look more closely at their workshops—the benches, the varieties and quality of the wood, the hand tools—in terms of the skill and sensitivity the students would like to develop. In so many schools, the woodshop is a low-priority matter as compared to the facilities for other crafts, except, perhaps, in terms of the mechanical equipment provided.

One wonders whether schools are as essential to crafts as they would like us to believe they are. A fair number of young people thinking about becoming woodworkers simply say, "Well, I've picked up some of the basic skills, I know a bit about wood and the equipment I'll need to work with wood, I have had a little experience, and now I'm wondering if I should go to a school at all." I find myself wanting to say to these young people, "No, I do not think you should go to a school, at least not a big school. Maybe the best thing would be to just start. Set up the simplest, least expensive shop you possibly can and then begin. Work. Start with the kind of things you can handle—tiny objects or kitchen interiors or repairs—and gather experience. Learn as you go along. Get an idea of what it is you can do well and what you like to do. What sort of person you are, really. On what scale you might want to work." It is important to have a clear picture of yourself in that respect so you won't get a great deal of expensive, large equipment and then find that what you really like to do is small, detailed work. Or the other way around. Someone might spend five years doing cabinetmaking and then discover that what he really wants to do, and could one day do well, is woodturning. So, it is necessary to simply try, and to look around and observe what other people are doing. Gather experiences—until a pattern emerges and things clear up. This is indeed a path some young people are choosing. They are willing, even eager, to go it alone, rather than be trapped in an institutional situation that will frustrate them.

That choice does, however, bring with it isolation: One *is* alone. And it is difficult to live and to work without friends, sharing, access to other people's experiences. One of the finest things that has begun to happen is that craftsmen inclined to self-discovery are beginning to get together. They tend to bump into one another, quite casually, almost by accident. A few people meet, and suddenly one person is saying to the other, "Hey, you live only twenty miles down the road from me. I didn't know you existed. I thought I was alone in these parts." Next thing you know these two people are talking, exchanging ideas, taking up practical problems: where to get wood, tools, machines, and so on. An exchange begins; it's like rings on the water. It is heartwarming to observe and enriching to participate in such contact. These craftsmen will continue to share, one thing will lead to another, and all those involved will benefit. There is a generosity, an openness among these people, and along with changing attitudes I see this as one of the most positive forces at work.

What we should try to avoid is the sort of neither/nor situation too many people get into: a low-cost shop, austere living quarters upstairs, hardly enough heating in either place. Not wanting to leave the shop even temporarily for bread-and-butter work, they have let themselves into doing almost anything for anybody who will pay for it. The shop is full of plywood, chipboard, formica, and the machines are taking a beating. There is very little (if any) nice, clean wood around. What tools one can see are simply hand tools, and they are experiencing the same unfair treatment as the machines. The craftsmen here are not happy about all this. They excuse the way things are, and talk about what they are really going to do when they get the chance. They are hopeful, and that is good. The only advice worth offering is: Keep your goal in mind. Get some fine wood in little bits and pieces, but get it. Put it away to dry properly. Improve the heating in the shop. And all the while think about finding or making some better tools. You'll need those fine tools to do that real work. So when the time comes and you get that chance, you will be ready.

Some Thoughts about Solid Wood

It is surprising how many of us, even after we have worked at our craft for quite a while, must pause now and then to consider a certain construction. We are often sidetracked by intricacies of shape and technical details and what is commonly called "design." In this maze we lose sight of some very basic facts about our material, wood, and how it can be put together into pieces of furniture. A few fundamental joints, such as the mortise and tenon, dovetail, frame (or post), and panel, have been used by craftsmen for hundreds, if not thousands, of years. They have stood the test of time and they have been used intuitively, artistically, or only methodically, in ways that fulfilled the intentions of craftsmen and the function of the pieces, for better or for worse. The many ways in which we later developed and redeveloped and varied these constructions is far beyond the range of my experience. They are almost infinite, especially now, when we are flooded with all sorts of technical aids and information and are getting a variety of views and usages and discussions on these topics. I think sometimes the variations and innovations are an end in themselves; they are a way of making it seem that we have found something new or have invented something all our own. This is seldom true. And even when it is true, being inventive at the expense of being sensitive may very well take us away from our best intentions and from the honest center of our craft.

When I visit exhibitions and look at various approved (or even acclaimed) pieces of woodworking, I can well imagine a show in which a skillful but mischievous cabinetmaker or woodworker would offer several pieces that in their intention—the proportions, and especially the shapes—were in tune with the times and the trends and the people who would be jurying the show and writing articles about the craftsmen and their work. But these pieces, at the same time as they would have a very striking visual appeal, would be deliberately made in a way that is at odds with the wishes of the wood itself. They would be, as an experiment or a joke, self-destructing pieces of furniture. They would not last long, but while they did last they would give the illusion of structural soundness.

Although it does not have the eyecatching appeal one would try to achieve in such an instance, the silver chest with its veneered surfaces and absence of end-grain edges will serve as an example. If I were to make a case that looked like this but the surfaces of which were, in fact, solid wood, it would be only a matter of time before the box began to self-destruct; with those horizontal, shaped pieces running the way they do and the solid flat surfaces firmly joined to them, something would just have to go. Thus we would have a good illustration of something that *looked* right, but was from the beginning wrong; and would presently reveal itself as such. Granted, one could invent all sorts of tricky ways to use solid wood throughout—I can hear the proposals for sliding-jointed rails and the like. They might work, yes. The point is, we would no longer have the same piece. The intended simplicity of the case itself (the rest is all but simple) would be lost. In relation to this, the result is contrived, we have a contradiction of purpose, which is another kind of what I call *wrongness*. Yet my bet is that the ploy would work. Alas, too little of the criticism and reporting about crafts and craft exhibitions nowadays provides us with the basis for a qualified, balanced evaluation. How often are we given a combination of aesthetics *and* purpose, function *and* judgment (or the lack of it) in workmanship, which means a total, not just visual, relationship to material and methods? All too rarely. We look so hard for originality; we might leave space in our search for a bit of reverence.

If a painter is an artist, a good critic should, I suppose, tell us about both the technical achievement and the artistic one—and let us judge from there. As regards literature, we want critics to tell us more about a book than the plot, number of pages, and personal life of the author. But when it comes to crafts—and this is particularly true of wood—the topic of sensitivity and feeling for workmanship, of real heart in the work itself, is seldom talked about. The gap between fine work and a fair evaluation of such work is a critical one. Some very important people (critics and others on whom we craftsmen depend) simply do not know enough about the media they present to the public. If they did, we would not have mushiness and mechanical mish-mash as a current ideal. We'd have some of it, yes; we always will. But it would be fairly balanced against other expressions, other values.

My own view—I dare call it a prediction—is that the evaluation, as it relates to the life and work of a craftsman and the response of an appreciative public, will be a central issue in the next few years. Something has changed, and whether we want to or not we will have to talk about this. And act. There is already a movement toward a quieter, richer expression in our craft; we who are concerned must find those who will help bring to wider attention a sense of what such work is about. There are people who would appreciate it, and respond, not *en masse*, but in some reasonable number, to the amount of fine work done. It isn't a question of the good guys against the bad guys. There are values, there is something called integrity. Grace, delicacy, warmth, power—these have been around for a long time. We could with their presence give a potential public a basis on which to evaluate and enjoy fine workmanship in contrast to the flamboyance and gaudiness that already abound.

As craftsmen we have, by and large, done a poor job of prompting a deeper evaluation. We get so caught up in details that we lose sight of more important things. After a show, or in a woodworking course, craftsmen often have long, heated, hold-or-not-hold arguments about grain direction and the strength or weakness of joints: "I do it this way and this way is right. This is how it has always been done," or "This is a completely new way of doing it, and what in the rules says this is not a better way?" Someone states that a certain construction absolutely won't hold, the answer comes: The piece has been together for seven years. Maybe in some circles seven years is a long time and what lasts seven years may last seventy or a hundred. On the other hand, it may not. Perhaps during those seven years the beginning of disintegration has already set in; it's just that it has not as yet become obvious. Snagged in the pros and cons of technicalities we forget the broader meaning of a method and its relationship to our material.

Perhaps if we ourselves become more sensitive and aware of the processes we do—the touches that give our work life, really—we could better communicate this to others. While learning how to do any basic procedure, for instance, we should also grasp—and be able to tell others—something about how it can be used in different situations, and how it should be modified to suit certain conditions.

There is, for example, no single quick, universal, completely obvious way of making a mortise and tenon. The clumsy one we do on a tradesman's level when making a workbench or a fence or a barn door is not the same joint we use when making furniture out of very hard wood, although "how-to" articles seldom point this out. The hardness of the wood calls for a greater accuracy because, unlike a soft wood, it will not yield to make up for small deviations. At the same time, hardness and all the other properties of the wood must be related to the delicacy, the refinement, or the intricacy of the piece as a whole.

As it is, we are in some places being offered an endless series of technical gymnastics, with no sense of progression, no reminder that most of the work can and should be done better. How is the person being fed such information ever to recognize—much less strive toward—more sensitive and satisfying expressions? Simplicity is at the heart of so much that is fine. How can we believe this when it is distorted to crudeness and then presented as fact?

All too often we are taught a basic technique or exercise without being given a clear sense of where it can lead. It's a "you-do-it-this-way" kind of thing, which may be all right for one person, but is a brake on another. If we are exposed to this attitude at an early stage of learning, and have no other point of reference against which to measure it, it is easy to see how we might come to believe that this is *the* way one does it, whereas it may be only a *part* of the way or *one* of many ways.

FACING PAGE: *The last silver chest, case and stand of spalted maple, drawers of bird's-eye maple. Height 80cm, width 55cm, depth 38cm. Oil finish. 1977. The piece is about 5cm higher than the few preceding ones done since I made the original in 1961.*

RIGHT: *One of the earlier versions, in Swedish maple, is more squat.*

Simplicity needn't be crude; it can, and should, include the sensitive. There is no good reason to keep saying that sensitivities, the fine points, must come much later. The ability to do them may come later, yes, but I believe the *awareness* that there are fine points, and what they are, should be implanted from the very start. Why should a novice not know that it is easier to work with a fine tool and a joyous hand than it is to rely on force? He may, despite this, use undue force with fine tools, out of lack of patience or just plain eagerness. But early in learning there should be an awareness that there is something better. "I'll show you an easy way to do it," we say. At first that is a relief and an aid—there is less to worry about. But the easiness is deceptive. We get bogged down in it; we form habits that do not allow for curiosity nor for a consciousness of the next level of skill, and the next. I'm speaking now of hand and eye and tools, over and above machines.

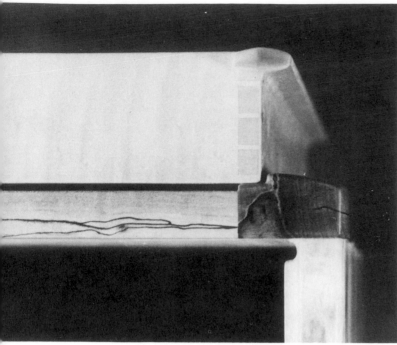

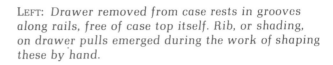

LEFT: *Drawer removed from case rests in grooves along rails, free of case top itself. Rib, or shading, on drawer pulls emerged during the work of shaping these by hand.*

View of silver chest showing veneered back set in rabbet and glued. The lip has a decorative purpose, and it enables the inside edges of the case to be rounded slightly.

LEFT: *Detail of case and one-piece siderail. Simplicity of construction is made possible through use of (sawn) veneered surface.*

I would like to imagine that if we show a beginner the rudiments of using a silversmith's hammer, we convey with it at least something of the need for light, relaxed taps and the resilient, effort-saving rhythm that is so important. Even if our beginner hits too hard, or in some other way wields the hammer incorrectly, he senses from what we have said about the art of this technique that there is a way of doing it better. If he wants to, he will sooner or later find that way. One day when the hammer starts to bounce lightly and pleasant things happen, he'll say, "Oh, so that's what the fellow meant!"

Ours is really a simple craft. But it is a rich one, too. At its best, the simple becomes obvious: a band of small discoveries, strung like pearls on a thread of curiosity, lending richness to our work.

I cannot help but wonder: Is there a connection between crudeness of hand and the overemphasis on technical points in our craft? Don't some of us get greater satisfaction from saving work than from actually doing it? True, the two can coincide, though more often we are faced with a choice; the result is apt to be an inner conflict, a condition undermining our self-confidence. A difficult part of teaching (or sharing experiences, really) is, I think, the need in some of us for a balance between a method we use and the satisfaction it can give. One may regard this as a matter of harmony and wholeness in work; for another it signifies only time wasted by self-preoccupation. And it is easy to say, "The reason why you're doing it explains what you get in return. Some people are technically inclined, others aren't. So what?"

All the same, I do remember instances where students were so distracted by the overemphasis on the technical aspects of certain things that they were unable to establish any personal relationship with the work they were doing. They wanted a real closeness to the process, but did not have the simple confidence needed to bring about this intimacy, let alone to make it an asset. They

were—and are—frustrated; they need encouragement. (Don't we all?) For them it is a help to hear that one should learn to relate properly to time: work is a fine part of living, and it includes looking at life. In our eagerness to get where we are going, we can devote so much attention to a map that we walk right past some of the things we had hoped to see and experience.

Admittedly, there are important technical realities in woodworking. And under certain conditions (Who establishes these? Do most of us choose, really?) it is silly not to take advantage of more or less foolproof methods. Besides, we do work for various reasons and in different ways. There definitely is a type of craftsman who is also a technician, and this person gets a lot out of solving problems along with handling the work. I have friends who can do wonders with an old machine; by the time they are through, it is better than new. Bob in New Jersey beams as he shows me his latest resurrection, an ancient joiner. "Listen to it hum. Sweet, eh? Come here; feel this crank. Go ahead, *feel* it. Isn't that nice?" Yes, it is; such things make even this old man happy.

A chap I know, who has studied in England, is now determined to set up a shop for fine-quality, small production furniture. He will do this very well, I'm sure; he has the knack for it, enjoys figuring out neatly rational methods while keeping a kind eye on the rest of the world. For those so inclined, there is confidence (and reward) in ways that are clearly marked.

But what about the many others? I have a haunting fear that for them the opposite is true: Technical certainties become almost a compulsion, creating a gap between them and the feeling they need of being *in* the work. Not only doing (directing) the work, but being in it; the difference here is very personal. One meets such students (or craftsmen) rather often, and it is dangerously easy to be unaware of how vulnerable they are in their naive eagerness, how easily distracted—even intimidated—by the technicalities which, for them, really should be secondary. These are observing people, perfectly capable of reasoning and straightforward methods—if left to do things without undue pressure. So let's not hustle them with efficiency, the need to perform. Let them get as close as they want to the wood they like. And choose their own tools, develop a feel for these, and work from there. To do this, we all need time. A point some of us should remember, and help each other toward, is the condition of undisturbed closeness to what we are doing. Very likely there is a critical stage before we develop the confidence not only to work harmoniously, as is right for us, but also to defend our way and the enjoyment it brings.

Defend. Why defend? It's rather revealing how the thought drifts in. . . . Maybe it is because I do not know enough; as a craftsman, I am rather uneducated, and not practical. This may bother some, but it can be reassuring to others. I suppose a few of you, like myself, don't know the exact specifications of the whetstones you use; I mean their grit and things like that. What you *sense* is that the one is fairly fine, it removes the marks of the grinding wheel but leaves a burr; the other does the rest of the work needed for a finished edge. Along the way are small secret satisfactions, such as noticing how not just the one stone, but a single part of it, an *area*, differs from the others, regardless of what the catalog and the specifications say. This corner of the stone is like glass, you feel it skid under the iron, whereas over there it cuts; your fingers sense this through the metal, you can hear the difference as you hone. And the meaning? Ah, yes, here may be where the defending comes in. What is the justification for pages of knowledge about how that edge looks under a microscope, say, if you can't sense when it is sharp and confirm this by a light stroke of the fingernail? Can you see, feel, hear how a shaving comes up out of a plane? Do you notice the cleanness in the burnished wake of a chisel cut? Sharpness has its test, the "flaw" that escapes your searching fingernail will not affect the surface left by a cutting tool on even a telltale wood like pear.

For me, there is satisfaction in such experiences. As there is in being able to see the logic of developing a feel for using a hand grinder, the kind of feel (easily arrived at) no amount of gadgetry can fully replace or really improve, because sharpening is in its essence a matter of touch. It's a relationship: the wheel, the rhythm with its live, light contact variable in an awareness of intention; it is, too, the *physical rightness* of the strokes we use to hone, the last flick on a particular part of a fine stone. Wait, that's not all. We will miss something unless we care enough about the way we tune our tool, and how we use it. Everything has to be there—or else we should be less than happy.

What is to be gained by breaking this everyday experience into scattered parts and discussing the fragments that only the touch of a caring hand can restore to the wholeness that is their meaning?

A few satisfactions are almost embarrassingly simple. Like noticing, as you try a first cut with a wooden plane left set as it was some days earlier, that the weather has changed. It's been raining, you have to tap the iron down a hair—and you find yourself smiling as you do so. . . .

"I went to Oistrakh's concert last night," my friend Jurg said to me, in Graz where he lives.

"Ah! Was it good?"

"Oh, yes. But . . . there was something, one could hear it, not just I, but those in the orchestra, too," Jurg looked at the sky. "We are going to get rain. . . ." A low, leaden sky confirmed what my violinist friend had *sensed* the evening before, in a crowded concert hall.

Of such moments are adventures made.

Using Solid Wood

For most of us a piece made entirely of solid wood has a recognizable ring. "Ah yes, solid wood," we say, and knock. The term *solid wood* is reassuring, akin to quality. Granted, it is a part of what should be good craftsmanship, it does have certain definite advantages. But there are disadvantages too, and these are less obvious to some of us. Which is regrettable, because using solid wood throughout is at times a limitation both technically and aesthetically. I'd like to emphasize the aesthetic aspect, because this is the area in which we are least aware of both limitations and possibilities.

Any fairly involved piece made of solid wood that is to be strong, and interesting, demands judgment on the part of the craftsman. The mere fact that it is solid wood does not in itself mean it is strong, much less that it is interesting. The idea that this might be so can be a trap. In making what should be an intricate or a delicate piece with many details, we sometimes get entangled in all sorts of unnecessarily complex constructions. Or, when we try to avoid the complicated, we often drift into oversimplicity or crudeness, which is another trap. Some of this crudeness is not our own fault, really. It happens because we are taught methods as we are taught the alphabet as a preliminary to literacy: Once we know *a* through *z* we are ready to start writing or reading. But even from *z* it can be a long way to expressing something our own.

During whatever process of learning, we need to respect our material. This is, I think, the basic requirement for being a craftsman in wood; even those of us who do not truly love wood can at least respect it. And we must be observant, and patient, and willing to work for what we aim to achieve. A simple idea may take us through a complex process; it often does just that. *We must be able to do the complex well, and yet arrive at, and preserve, simplicity.* Simplicity is the beginning of many fine things. A childish verse or peasant's song can become, through the creative force of the right person, the theme for a movement in a symphony. With our craft, as with music, we have to know how the various instruments work, and how they sound, before we can begin to make music.

When using solid wood exclusively, I think the most important thing is that the resulting piece convey a true sense of solid wood. Granted, this means being able to judge the essence of such work without becoming ensnared in the trivial or the irrelevant. Some of us hope that with help from those who care and have a perspective on the craft, a reasonable basis on which we can do and appreciate such work will evolve. As it is, there is some confusion about solid wood, as well as about good workmanship when using it. The past serves as both a good and a bad example. We contemplate work done long ago and nod, saying, "It was done right in those days." Sometimes, yes. But only sometimes.

Primitive means, rather crude tools, and often no machines forced the craftsman into a close relationship to his material. There was a certain directness of method—so far, so good. What was obviously wrong usually (though not always) revealed itself, often with serious consequences for the craftsman, who in the past was more directly responsible for his work than some of us are today. But then, as now, the result did depend on a person. We have old things, even prized antiques that are, if we judge them strictly, shoddy work. Yes, there is even gross misuse of material in some of those old pieces: bottoms and backpieces glued or pegged onto a permanent perimeter; chair seats of solid wood fastened to legs and backpieces in a way that, through the years, encourages them to crack apart; drawer bottoms with the grain running with, rather than across, the action of the drawer itself. Ignorance, carelessness, even dishonesty have always been among us. Then, as now, one had to consider a lot of things as he worked. But nowadays, with all the information from the past plus the chance to make (or get) refined tools and to use certain handy aids when justified, we have less excuse for making errors.

Work done in solid wood need *not* be heavily dimensioned (to convince us it is durable), nor do the various constructions, especially the joints, have to be obvious and visible. They can be; certainly a nicely made joint is a pleasure to behold. At the same time, there is a temptation to make them eye-catching, which may lead to overemphasizing them, giving a clumsiness—sometimes called a "whimsical touch"—to the piece. The result does not really coincide with our intentions and degree of sensitivity, but is a kind of subconsciously enforced exhibitionism. Our use of constructions should be easily discernable when that is the natural thing and fits the piece. At other times, however, we should resist the temptation and remind ourselves: It is even more satisfying to plan and make a sound, pleasing construction in solid wood that has subtlety and a fine relationship to the rest of the piece. It will still express a sense of solid wood. Will anyone notice? One hopes so. I think that when we see things nicely weighted and crafted we will tend to experience them in the way they were intended. We may even learn to appreciate them more because they are modestly done than we would if they were made in an aggressive way.

For the present, much of the thinking and talk about cabinetmaking is concentrated on its techniques, the usages of various constructions, their absolute rights and wrongs. Too little attention is given to relating these to the piece as a whole. We are not given enough with which to judge, but only fragments. Often these are showy fragments that by their technical content impress people.

Fitting parts of wood together and relating these to a purpose is one aspect of making furniture. A pity, though, if building appears to be the only task—and too often it is all that seems to matter to some of us. Going about it in such a one-sided way, we can end up with something less than we hoped for. As we plan and do this work, we could be taking into account other details yet to come, such as the structural and *visual* role of the various dimensions of the wood we use. Thickness, for instance, deserves consideration.

How thick a piece of wood will be is usually decided in terms of its part in the construction of the piece. True, but that is not all there is to it. Thicknesses and the way we use them help to determine the *character* of the piece as well. By and large, many of us are not aware enough of what various dimensions mean, except as numbers. And they are rather vague and uninteresting measurements at that—one inch, three-quarters, five-eighths, one-half inch, and so forth. Often these are related to wood as we buy it in standard thicknesses; we mill them and use them in dimensions that echo the sizes they came in. There is, of course, a practical reason for this: To some, resawing is regarded as extra work taking extra time. I hope this attitude will change.

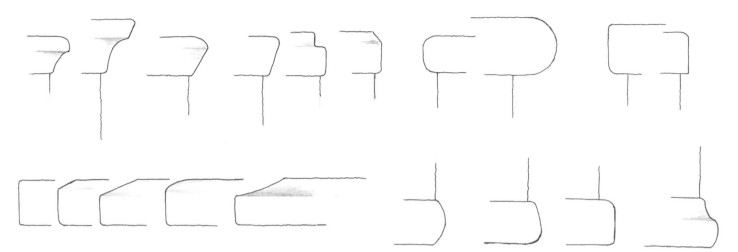

Imaginary edges: A few ways of conveying the intention of hard, soft, thick, thin—only a beginning....

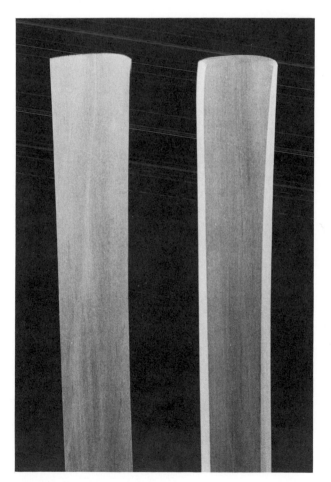

Two views of top of leg for music stand in natural pearwood: Piece on the left in each photo has not yet been shaped; piece on the right in each shows the hand-shaped details, which seem to affect the dimensions themselves.

Let me remind you that sensitivity to small differences in dimensions is very important. Not only does the actual thickness of the wood matter (along an edge, for example), but also the visual message of the thickness, how the eye experiences it. We can have a top, bottom, or sidepiece three-quarters of an inch thick for structural reasons and then, by doing things—often very little things—to an edge or corner, we change the way that thickness meets the eye and the way it feels. The edge can be made to seem a trifle thinner, but still clearly defined and with a hardness in it that suits the wood—that really comes from the wood—and, in turn, suits the piece. Or we can make that same edge quite a bit thinner and soft, if a feeling of softness pleases the rest of the piece and our intention. So we have this visual asset: We can alter a dimension in terms of its visual impression while maintaining its size for reasons of strength. We do not have to run to the joiner or planer to mill down a piece because its edge seems too thick. We have other means, if we just notice them, of changing that

Wall cabinet, spalted maple. Height 72cm, width 24cm, depth 11cm. Oil finish. 1978. I wanted a visual sense of refinement, thin borders and modest shadings. To achieve this and still make the carcass strong, I had to dovetail the inner top and bottom pieces (see detail) and set the door into cabinet sides slightly.

edge. This becomes more apparent as we work with hand tools. Here I mean fine, clean-cutting tools. It is amazing how the feel of a particular piece of wood changes as we work it—a rounded or beveled edge done with plane or spokeshave actually grows there before us. We experience the real difference between a little, more, and still more. A curved piece assumes still another tension as we work an edge. It is not dead-even, as with a router; but we develop a hand-and-eye relationship to that shape and its meaning as we feel it should be. Granted, we do have to care and have fine tools and learn to see. I mean really *see* what we are doing. And, of course, we have to learn to feel as well.

Cabinet made of the same wood (spalted maple) but with a different intention. The door has a lip on either side and opens from right to left. Height 78cm, width about 22cm, depth 11cm. Oil finish. 1978.

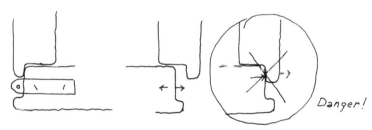

Danger!

I believe that in the course of time dimensions as numbers decrease in importance. It is the way a piece of wood feels in our hands, how we measure and experience it by eye and touch, that really matters. It should matter not only to us, but to others as well. The illustrations perhaps do not convey the true sense of difference between various thicknesses nor how they affect shapes and then relate to a given piece by accentuating certain details and toning down others, but do not let my shortcomings put you off. Take a few pieces of wood and practice, observing what happens. Do it again. Do it by eye and by touch: See, and feel with your fingers; touch is almost as important as sight. Most of us like to stroke wood, follow obvious shapes, and talk of sensuality. Let's enjoy *sensitivity* as well, small subtleties that are not separate from sensuality, but are a part of it and add to the richness of our experience.

So do practice. Hold wood of a certain thickness between two fingers, close your eyes, guess at its size. Work it a little thinner, and try again. Likewise, close your eyes and feel slight curves and all sorts of shaped edges.

Rushing through life as we do, we are at odds not only with time, but with our senses as well. It seems we have to go back to a childlike state and try to experience things in a straightforward, unpremeditated way, as nature surely intended us to do. Why are we so calculating? Why do we try so hard to get around the simple approach and those natural beginnings of sensitivity?

Take the time to discover subtleties. Look at your wood, feel it, listen with your mind to its many-sided message. One day when you need it you will remember something of this special kind of awareness. I hope it will enhance the results and the enjoyment of your work!

The way a door fits a cabinet—how it joins the sides and how it pivots—is a classic example of the pairing of function and decoration. And the order of these should be function first, decoration second. Some tragicomic mistakes result from not having those priorities ordered; right and wrong reveal themselves, often too late.

Not long ago, a friend sent me a sample knife hinge now on the market. By their very nature, knife hinges are extremely strong. Thus, they can be finely proportioned, discreetly decorative. Besides, and equally important, they allow for a greater variety of door positions, both open and closed, and they encourage more subtle relationships of door to cabinet side or front than do butt hinges. There can be gentle shadings or bold accentuations that lend their touch to the piece. Yet these hinges my friend sent quite frankly disappointed me. They worked, yes, but the relationship between function and decoration was off, the balanced dimensions and neatness that should typify such hinges was lacking. The dimensions, for example, were coarse, the holes countersunk for unnecessarily large screws. Whoever made them was not close enough to subtle work, did not understand that knife hinges, when used properly, exert hardly any pull on the screws, nor are they apt to twist loose, the way butt hinges do. Anyone who understood that would know a proportionately smaller screw hole would have worked *and* looked more pleasing.

We craftsmen are partially to blame for such, and even greater, distortions. Many of us regard hinges as simply a means by which to swing a door; our thinking about doors in general is crude, or at least out of scale.

Being so accustomed to using knife hinges, I am apt to oversimplify an account of how I fit them. Along with their advantages are peculiarities too. Here are a few points to keep in mind:

The relationship between the pivot point and the edge of the door (with straight hinges it is the outside; with L-shaped ones, the front) determines whether or not the door will open at all (a worthy consideration!), and if it does, how it will pivot. The amount the pin protrudes, or is pulled in, should be equal on both parts of the door. Any difference will be *doubled* as the door swings. What starts as a good fit with the door closed ends up as lopsidedness when it opens.

Equally important: The distance between the straight type of hinge (and its pin) and the front edge of the cabinet side must be equal all around. Otherwise, the door ends up askew in a certain (usually open) position. Again, the error is doubled. And neither of these common errors can be corrected by other, half-errors, however well intended.

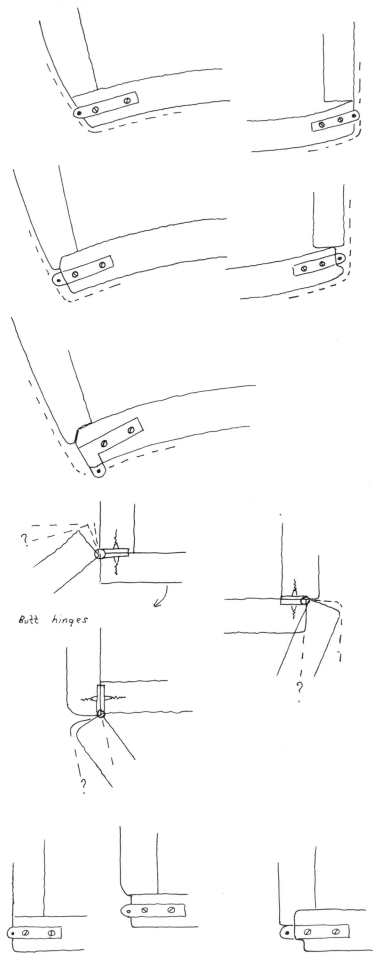

Door and hinge of concave showcase cabinet (shown on page 128). Having no lip, this door swings farther on pivot than the one pictured on page 27.

Back of maple wall cabinet: Brass keyhole fitting for wall-hung cabinets is easy to make.

Butt hinges

A good fit begins with properly locating the hinge parts that fit into the cabinet case itself. As some of you know, I do not complete the carcass before making the door or doors. Rather, I try to weave these together in ways I will explain later (see my discussion of Composing). Let me just say here that I dry-clamp the case and make a first tight fit of the door in order to check the width and how I want the door to meet the cabinet, and whether there is any warpage or wind. The case must be clamped tightly *as it will be when glued.* Then, if there is any wind, it can be noted and marked on the two diagonally opposite corners that are tight. I usually note exactly how much should be removed at each of these (half the total wind). With two doors, fit straight and true along the middle before you look for wind; otherwise, later on, the corrections will involve changing the thickness of one or both doors. Avoid this!

You notice I take a small amount of wind for granted. Theoretically, all parts of a cabinet should line up. Actually, they seldom do completely, especially when one is working with solid wood, and perhaps coopered doors. The human element is present in such work—learn to control and enjoy it.

Whatever the type of hinges, we must, in addition to locating the one part properly in the carcass, fit its other half correctly to the door. It is possible to make small final corrections, but with L-type hinges the possibility is limited since the shoulder of the hinge corresponds to the outside edge of the door. That can be an advantage or a disadvantage. Laterally, there is only one position where a door and its L-hinges fit. That means the corresponding parts in the cabinet case have to be placed absolutely accurately; we cannot hope to shift them even a trifle. Besides, these hinges are usually used with a door that is pulled in a bit, or set at a particular angle (see drawings). As regards in-depth fit—that is, how snugly the door will fit the cabinet sides—this is decided once and for all by the position of the pins to the front edge of each door at the corners.

Fitting door and hinges: Cabinet dry-clamped, door fitted snugly.

Planning for placement of hinge: Spacer relates to thickness of door and final position of hinge. The spacer piece shown on the door shows a first orientation only.

The line corresponds to the inside edge of the hinge, the contours of which will be marked accordingly, with the pin in the desired relation to the outside of the cabinet (or box or whatever).

Straight hinges are another matter; we can make a last sideways adjustment by filing the hinge end; as the hinge slips farther into the mortise, the door moves sideways out, not in, as one may at first imagine. And if you correct one hinge only, the door tilts accordingly.

Finally, you can't back a hinge out without having to patch the door (terrible thought!). Therefore, start with that part of the hinge a hair farther out than the final location you desire (a pair of doors will then fit "too tightly" at the middle). Cautiously work the hinge in and the door out until you get a proper fit.

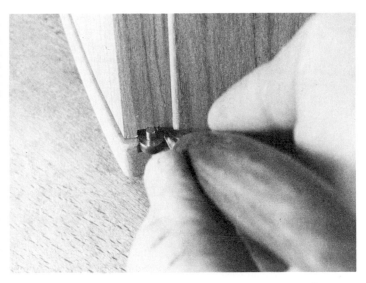

ABOVE: *The bottom hinge with washer. The door has been planed a trifle short to allow it, when finally hung, to be lifted by the thickness of the washer; the result will be a free swing. Here a first cut (notch) is made to allow positioning of the door even if this means overlapping a part of the pin. With the door in position, final accurate marks are made with a thin-bladed knife. It is vital to note the relationship of the door edge to pivot pin; that is, whether, and how much, the door overlaps this.*

TOP RIGHT: *Door with hinge outlined roughly (for purpose of illustration), and the knife marks that reveal a final slight correction. The notch on the door edge, corresponding to the thickness of the hinge, has been scribed and then chiseled carefully.*

BOTTOM RIGHT: *Marking boundaries (contour) of hinge with a sharp knife and straightedge. If the straightedge has coarse sandpaper on its underside it will not slip. Relation of pivot pin to side edge of door has been taken into account.*

Let us memorize.

Straight hinges: protrusion of pin at side edge determines lateral position of door.

L-shaped hinges: shoulder flush with door edge at corner; relation of pin to front edge now decisive for forward-back (i.e. in-depth) fit.

As you see in the drawings, I make mortises in the doors by hand, having scribed and notched for hinge thickness and then marked the contours with a sharp knife. I do the same with the fits in the carcass, although it is quite possible to use a hand router here if the template is accurate. Make trial cuts to check the depth, and get used to locating the template exactly.

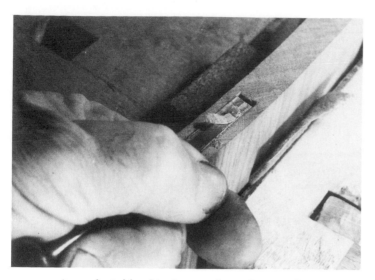

A comfortable chisel ground to a low angle and made razor sharp. It is held short so the hand serves as a stop (as does the notch at far end). The first cuts are with a narrow (⅛") tool; for the final clean-up, a wider one is better.

These are only pointers. It is best to do your own thinking—before, not after, you get into trouble! Try working with a simple drawing or even cardboard templates of door and hinge, the better to see how they will fit and work. Study the possibilities. Practice various solutions. It is important to understand what will happen in a given situation. Some of you will work out your own variations, and it would not surprise me if still newer types of hinges are developed. Many craftsmen are inventive with metal as well as wood. It is feasible to make very neat, strong hinges to suit the exact purpose of the piece one wants to build. For those who can't custom-make hinges, I hope really fine knife hinges will soon be available commercially.

A fair fit. How we treat an edge, corner, or surface can convey a sense of hard or soft, subtle shading or bold overlapping—each in relation to the feel of the wood and the mood of the piece. Cabinet here is of lemonwood, and it has two doors.

Let's take another look at a single door fitted to a cabinet. You will notice that when the cabinet sides have rabbets the door can move only within the limits of the two shoulders. Therefore, it is important to take into account the amount of expansion and contraction the door might develop. Yes, there is a danger in a solution such as this. At the same time, with the possibilities it offers for soft shadings and decorative vertical grooves serving as finger grips, there is a certain advantage as well. Another, safer variation would be a door with a lip along each front edge, simply set against the cabinet and pulled in a little.

Other safe ways of fitting a single door can be tried. The door may rest against the two front edges of the sides, either flush with the outside or pulled in to form a slight shading (step) there. Such a door can expand and contract freely in one direction—that is, away from the hinges. There will be variance in the overlap or shading along the edge that does not pivot, whereas the edge with the hinges will remain constant. In a door ten or twelve inches wide, made of fairly hard dry wood, this give-and-take will not be irritating. When the door is not pulled in at the sides, but is left flush with them, the door is experienced as a continuation of the sides, although sometimes not quite flush with the one side because the door width will vary seasonally. A detail that can be disturbing here is that the visible grain on the edge of the door is apt to be flat, whereas the grain on the cabinet side is preferably vertical; the result is a conflict of pattern. A single door is fairly easy to fit. It's important to remember that even a slight wind in a door is often difficult to correct; as I mentioned earlier, one is better off repeating this wind in the cabinet sides when they are of solid wood.

With two doors we have to do a bit more thinking. Usually they meet at the middle, where they overlap; the right-hand door with its lip, as a rule, overlaps the left-hand one, which has a rabbet. Such flat doors forming one plane are not much of a problem. But with convex or concave doors

we should remember two principal points: Concave doors fit properly in only one specific position. If pushed in farther than that they leave one another; the fit quickly becomes too loose. Convex doors, similarly, are meant to form a particular curve and fit in only one position. They will be too tight if pushed inside that position; outside it—at a wider curve—they are too loose.

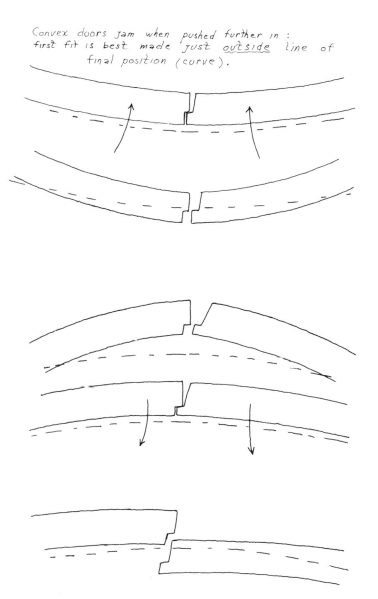

Convex doors jam when pushed further in: first fit is best made just outside line of final position (curve).

Concave doors become tighter – jam – and then overlap as they come outward. Make first fit on or slightly inside intended line (or curve).

These changes begin when the doors are only slightly out of line. And they increase very rapidly. This means that beyond the desired position of the door there will be variations difficult or even impossible to correct. As with hinges, it's wise to make templates of the doors, and to fit these to the cabinet case or the drawing. Think and rethink, because very much is at stake. I find it a help and precaution to fit convex doors first just *outside* the desired curve, knowing this is the safe side, since it allows for final adjustments. Once the hinges are on, I can push in the doors an eighth of an inch or so and they will fit tightly, if that is what I want. Or I can achieve the desired space between them with a certain margin of safety. Likewise with concave doors, I suggest you make a preliminary fit slightly *inside* the final curve, hang them, then pull them outward a little to make that fit.

Two doors consisting of frame and panel (or glass) present another problem: One must consider not only how the frames will fit where they meet, but also how their width together relates to the rest of the frame parts, the judging of which involves the piece as a whole. You see, we are making more than just doors.

Although we sometimes do find two doors simply butted together, it is far better to overlap them nicely along that middle line. To achieve the overlap, however small, we will have to alter the width of one or both of the frame parts involved. That is one consideration. Another is the actual visible width we want at the middle, how it balances against the other elements of the doors *and* against the piece as a whole. It should be obvious that the two verticals toward the middle should together be less than twice the width of their outside counterparts; otherwise, the result is very awkward. (Alas, the obvious doesn't always serve as a warning.) We'll be changing the width of these parts at the center, first to nearly what we want, and then further to form the overlap by making a lip on one and a rabbet on the other. There are various ways of handling these fits; the illustrations are only to help

in the direction which best suits your way of thinking and seeing. What's most important is to get things straight in your head, to start right.

You can choose to begin with the four vertical members of equal width (this makes milling and sawing the joints easier) and then, after gluing, to cut these parts narrower, working by stages to the desired fit, including the neat overlap. I have a shaper bit with rounded corners for this.

Alternatively, you might want to make all the parts as close as possible to final size, leaving only a small margin for the overlap itself. Fine, if you can manage it, but it's somewhat scary. Any slight miscalculation can be fatal, and it is amazing how a series of tiny discrepancies, each so human, connive to result in a poor fit.

I usually have a measuring stick (simply a straight strip of any wood cut to suitable length) to help me along; the less numbers flying about, the better. Unless the various frame parts are to differ greatly in final width, I'd suggest using only one width in our exercise—or at least keeping the four vertical pieces the same—and sawing the joints accordingly. Although it is not directly our topic, I should remind you to make the necessary rabbets or grooves for panels or glass before gluing up. Do this neatly and with care—it pays! (See *Showcase Cabinets*.)

With the frames glued and trimmed to a first generous square (don't be too eager about that final fit!), we continue our thinking:

If we rabbet the left-hand piece for the overlap and then in its right counterpart make a slightly deeper lip by a rabbet on the inside, we reduce the visible part of the left member by the width of the rabbet. This will affect both grain pattern *and* the visible part of the frame widths. We will be left feeling the one is too wide and the other is too narrow—which, in fact, is true. With any reasonably refined work this discrepancy is really disturbing. In some cases, especially with very hard woods having a calm pattern of grain, one can make a slight groove or marking in the right-hand door corresponding to the inner (hidden) edge of the lip. As the doors overlap, we will experience a double line there. This can create a refined effect in some sophisticated pieces.

Generally, however, it is better to do one of two other things. We can reduce the width of the right-hand doorframe by the width of the rabbet or groove that we are going to make in the left-hand door. Thus, after we have fitted the doors and have the overlap, the visible part of each door-half will be equal. They will then be narrower, that is true; but they will be *equally* narrower, by the amount of the overlap, which in most instances is something between three-sixteenths and one-quarter of an inch.

Another solution is to leave both halves of the door equal at first, then to glue a thin piece to the inside edge of the left-hand door and machine it to form the desired rabbet. Now we have the same overlap, the same simple, calm fit of the doors as before, with the difference that the doors retain their original equal width. This only sounds complicated; with a bit of concentration the whole matter can be clearly settled in your mind, after which these various solutions become habit and you are free to make your own variations of door fits.

The purpose of all this is to keep the work under control, to know what size door or doors you want, and then to make them that size with the least amount of effort and worry.

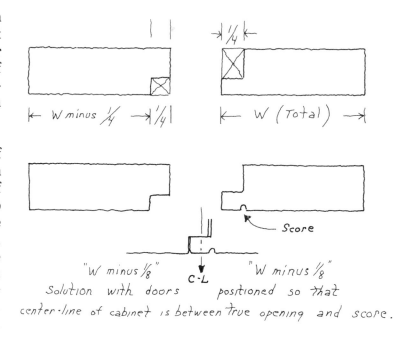

Solution with doors positioned so that center-line of cabinet is between true opening and score.

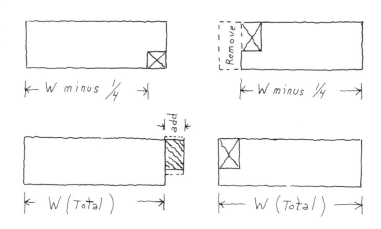

"Real" Veneer

Craftsmen who use commercial veneer do so for various different reasons, some of which we don't always talk about. Sometimes the use is justified, sometimes it is not. But for the experienced eye there is often a particular air about such work. I can only describe it as *dryness*. The veneered surface is lacquered because it is so terribly thin; it won't take some of the nicer finishes we use elsewhere. One senses the artificiality of those pretty surfaces, so perfectly matched. . . .

Along with this we have the techniques and habits of working with veneer. They lead to a lack of friendliness in the work; to hard edges where veneer meets veneer or sharp, mitered edge gluings. The whole thing is not unlike a for-the-market product, even if it did come from a craftsman's workshop and is marked "handmade." No wonder the word *veneer* has a bad sound nowadays.

It was not always so. At the cabinetmakers' school I attended we did a good deal of work involving veneer: We were assigned to build a fashionable and elegant writing desk bearing the name "Nefertiti" and an oval sewing table, "Frida," with a delicate inlaid border of flowers made of lemonwood. And when the time came for several of us to do our apprentice piece, someone always chose that sober cabinet called "The Middle Kingdom," with its rosewood parquet surfaces.

The veneer press we had at that time consisted of iron-bound wood beams, about five by eight inches, forming a frame with iron screws tightened by means of a heavy key. Sheets of masonite and wide planks were placed between the work and the screws. For certain work we had one-eighth-inch zinc plates; these we warmed and used with hide glue. All this and more belong to the process of veneering: the concern when making glue, the tense hurrying at the press, the waiting (often overnight), then the opening of the press to see the result. Yes, there was something special about it all. The veneer we had then was thicker than what we can obtain nowadays. Often it had been sawn, albeit commercially, rather than having been cut by knife. We were told about how old-timers made their own solid wood core. Some of us used such solid cores—there was lots of work to it—with or without a diagonal intermediate layer of sapele veneer to lock the grain. Mostly we had the commercial solid block stock, which consisted of fir staves and abaci cross-bond. The best variety was a German quality product with abaci core and sapele cross-layers. It came in thicknesses from ten millimeters and on up to over twenty-five millimeters (one inch) thick. For thinner work we used masonite core or, better yet, layers of birch plywood from Finland—very fine grade—which was obtainable from one millimeter and on up. For a long while veneer, for me, was associated with these experiences, with quality work and enjoyment.

We had an intarsia saw there at the shop, made of an old foot-operated sewing machine. I remember sawing those little flower patterns of all kinds of rare woods. Sometimes you dropped a piece on the floor and, if you had not swept before beginning to saw these precious, irreplaceable pieces, it was down there, hidden somewhere among the shavings. At best, you spent some time crawling around looking for it. Otherwise, the flower, or perhaps several flowers, had to be redone. That experience served as a reminder to sweep the floor before starting to saw.

Later on, in my own shop, I had a veneer press that consisted of three screw-clamp yokes similar to the ones we had had at the school, but smaller. And, of course, there was my fine bandsaw. Several of the pieces that I conceived during those early years were done with the help of sawn veneer.

Lately, things have changed. And I don't think the changes have been only for the better. We have our trust in commercial veneer, we are into a whole process that, even in a small workshop, is similar to the methods used in a factory. So in the crafts sense, veneering is not what it used to be. Still, there are a few striking exceptions where veneered work is very much alive. Let's hope we get more of it.

We can and should make our own veneer, and out of the best wood. One obvious reason to use veneer primarily in a piece of furniture is if we have just a little bit of a particularly rare wood and we want to get the most out of it by using it where it really shows. That's a good reason, with this reservation: Try to resist the temptation of making the parts with your rare wood more important than the rest of the piece. Avoid letting it jump out and wave, "Look! a curiosity," leaving us with only this to remember about the work you have done.

Another urge to veneer comes through an awareness of the flexibilities allowed by this technique. We may wish to achieve an effect that should and will be different from that of solid wood only. We might make a box or a cabinet case with veneer because our basic intent is a calmness, a subtlety of detail that cannot be gained otherwise. Used this way, veneer gives us not only stable surfaces, but also edges where we can work with sensitive touches. With it we can achieve a refinement that doesn't go with end grain and other characteristics typical of constructions involving solid wood only. Remember also that with stable (veneered) stock, we are free to choose the direction of grain on any given surface. Using it properly, we can achieve certain definite results in an honest and pleasing way. The entire piece—cabinet or whatever—need not be veneered. We may combine solid wood parts with certain veneered surfaces. There are at times good reasons for wanting to do this. For instance, we have a solid wood case with its strong construction and then, because we do not want the frame-and-panel solution for the backpiece, we choose to veneer this. Even if a frame and panel can be made rather subtle with small shadings and neat profiles, it is not the unbroken surface that we may want in that particular instance. Besides, although a frame-and-panel construction is fairly sturdy, there are practical reasons why a veneered surface as a backpiece or a bottom is even more appropriate. For one thing, it is stronger, since this part, being completely stable (there is no change in size with varying humidity) can be glued into place. This, in turn, lends great stability to the rest of the piece.

Even if a frame-and-panel construction is generally the most decorative and finest way to make a stable door for a cabinet, at times when one wants a more austere, unbroken wood surface, veneer could be used. But we use it with a soft, friendly feeling; because our veneer is fairly thick we can work the surfaces as we wish and then apply the kind of finish we think really does justice to the wood.

We can also use edge gluings thick enough to round nicely. It is surprising what just a slight rounding of an edge will do, how it differs from a sharp edge and becomes friendly both to eye and to touch. Furthermore, with a veneered surface that is about two millimeters (3/32") thick one can have the edge gluing inside—that is to say, under—the veneer itself, and then give soft edges to that surface, which appears whole and unbroken.

Even with subtleties a good craftsman still wants sound constructions. Maybe I should point out something here: It is ridiculously easy for some of us to get confused about what is stable and what is not, in which direction a certain piece of wood will move—that is, if it is to move at all. We don't mix solid wood and veneered surfaces in the case itself. We do not, for instance, make cabinet sides of solid wood and add a veneered top and bottom. Whether solid or veneered, all four parts around any perimeter should be the same. So should any partitions, shelves, and drawers between them.

Following are glimpses of various steps in a process of making and using veneer. Study them, ask yourselves questions, and imagine various situations in which you can take advantage of veneer in these or more fanciful ways. Notice how, when we have a particularly rare piece of wood with an interesting pattern, we can cut away a width from the solid piece before we saw the veneer itself and later use strips of this as our edge gluings. These will then be a harmonious part of the surface in both pattern and quality. This would be a special instance, and calls for a bit of pick-and-poke. We usually do have extra pieces of wood from which we can saw our edge gluings that are in grain and color fairly close to the surface we have produced.

Fitting and gluing together the various pieces of veneer to form a surface is not too difficult, and it is rather pleasant work. I first make up each surface, gluing the pieces edge to edge, and then attach it to the core (or base) either with tape or with two very small brads placed outside the usable surface. This ensures that the parts do not slip out of place while being glued and pressed.

Most often I use the veneer as I have sawn it—two or two and a half millimeters (about 3/32") thick, up to seven inches wide—and do not run it through the planer at all. This works very well because my bandsaw is so fine and the thicknesses are even. One can, of course, run sawn veneer through a planer, but it's rather tricky and the percentage of loss through splitting and various other troubles in the machine is apt to be high. So if you are going to surface the veneer after sawing, do saw quite a bit more of it than you will actually need. As for glue, in all but a few cases I use ordinary yellow or white glue for veneering. After taking the piece out of the press, I place it on edge somewhere in the shop and let it rest for a day or two. As a rule, there is little or no warpage; I have not had trouble with pieces glued this way.

Several years ago I gave away my three veneer presses, or frames. Since then I have done little work involving veneer. It's not one of my favorite techniques, though a few of my favorite pieces are done this way. I think that, used properly, veneer has certain advantages, among them added structural strength, unbroken calm (or patterned) surfaces, and freedom of direction. Further,

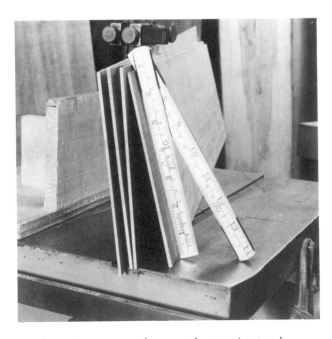

Bandsawing pearwood veneer for music stand.

a properly done veneered surface is stable; it has no give-and-take, will warp very little or not at all. Last, but not least, veneer properly sawn and properly used by the craftsman is not a substitute, a similar but inferior wood; it is actually *the* wood out of which we are making something meaningful, it is something for which we don't want to make any excuses.

These then are definite advantages. And I'm afraid that not enough thought is being given to them, to the use of "real" veneer when such use is justified, because all too many craftsmen associate veneer with commercial products and a usage that is less than enjoyable. Ordinary, commercial veneer *is* uninteresting, and the whole step-by-step process of using it is certainly uninspiring. Nonetheless, we still have this dry, I would say heartless, use of veneer by craftsmen. Which is a pity, because once we solve a few problems here we are really on the way toward interesting possibilities which will show our feeling for wood, our fantasy, and honest workmanship. Admittedly, with veneer we lose some of the charm of total solid wood; on the other hand, we should know enough to use veneer when the idea of a piece justifies it, and to use it in a way that is in itself alive and interesting. What we forfeit by using other than solid wood only, we gain through the proper use of veneer. It is then that "real" veneer is honestly wood.

We must experiment, develop our own techniques and variations, use judgment, and balance function and fantasy to achieve a consistency about the piece as a whole. I don't think one should try to work with this kind of veneer in large surfaces. One by two or three feet is fairly close to my limit. Smaller pieces are even better. There the rare pattern of a wood, nice proportions, simple lines, and the unbroken surfaces of veneer are completely at home.

Spalted maple for silver chest. Surfaces will be of three widths. Pieces removed before sawing veneer are for the edge-gluings to come later.

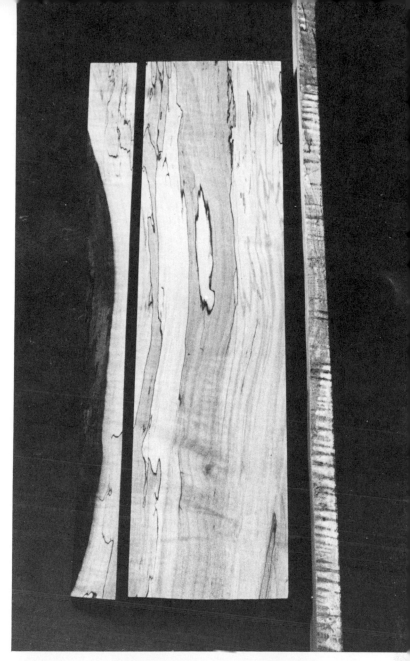

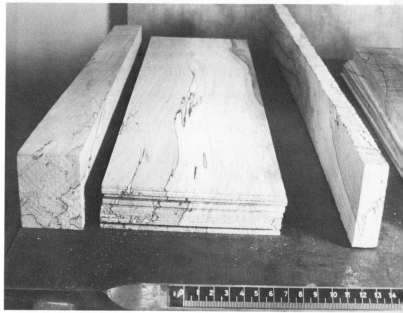

Once we have mastered certain simple constructions using veneer and high-quality solid core base material, we can form our surfaces as we choose. The veneer can have its grain lengthwise when it suits our purpose—for example, to work with a certain proportion—or it can be laid the other way, or in several directions (as a parquet) when both grain and color pattern call for this.

There are so many possibilities to play with: proportions, shadings, colors. Remember, too, that we needn't hide the end grain on edge gluings. Why miter the corners when those little squares or rectangles of darker end grain on the edge gluings can be used so decoratively? In a smaller piece (a jewelry box or such), we are apt to have all the parts veneered—the case, lid, bottom, everything. Our freedom then is great. We

Hand-planing veneer edges: The fit should be snug along the entire length.

Underside of surface (this one is maple) needs to be cleaned along joints before being glued onto both sides of high-quality cross-bonded solid core.

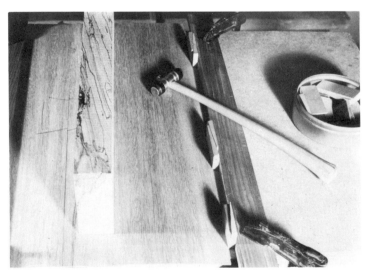

Gluing veneer widths to form a surface (here doussie for top of showcase cabinet): Straight-edged pieces clamped to chipboard "table," paper under area to be glued; low-angle wedges used in pairs exert a firm, even pressure.

Veneer, cross-bond layers (barely visible because of saw marks), and solid wood core. Part of the piece removed before the veneer was sawn has been put back in place, producing an apparently whole surface.

Basic construction of silver chest, veneered and solidly doweled.

Side of silver chest showing pieces inserted for along-the-grain run of drawer.

Front is edge-glued, but corners have not yet been softened by rounding.

Finished side with pattern of wood almost undisturbed.

can do the same with a cabinet or similar case, but these surfaces may tend to appear monotonous. Veneered doors and backpieces have their visual limitations, which weigh against certain structural advantages. There is a lot of unbroken surface; unless the wood is especially suited in terms of pattern, it will not account for itself.

The person most apt to be interested in making and using veneer is one who is aware of small, unusual pieces of wood and tends to gather these. Study all the wood you intend to use. Observe whether it is sound or not. Often striking pieces are also the ones with checks, knots, fungus, the beginning of rot, and other faults or dangers. Judge how much of the wood is usable. If it is to be veneer, allow generously for bandsaw cuts and surfacing. I think you should also, if possible, have veneer for one or two surfaces extra, as a precaution.

Before you select and saw veneer, ask yourself what it is you want to achieve. How will the surfaces of the carcass or other parts of the piece relate to, let us say, the doors and backpiece? What about the stand or visible drawer fronts? Work this out in your mind. First in terms of color and pattern, then as a practical problem of portioning out enough and a bit more material for each part of the piece. Study the wood to be sawn as veneer. Observe the pattern on each side. Notice on the ends how the colors or lines shift: Your veneer will have the character of both those outside surfaces plus something in between these, which you cannot quite predict. That's part of the adventure. And the danger.

With veneer, perhaps even more than with solid wood, it is vital that every piece is properly dried. Here warpage is disastrous. So use dry wood! Have your bandsaw blades sharp and as thin as possible. Make a practice cut or two in some other wood before sawing the precious veneer itself. Surface very little or not at all if you want the patterns to flow easily into each other as you later join the various widths of veneer together. Of course, with a simple surface of

doussie or mahogany everything is easier— the wood is predictable, you can relax more. But with eccentric wood, it's a risky business, though quite thrilling in its challenge.

Whatever the wood, fit and glue the widths carefully. Do not spring the joints! Keep the edges flush on the underside. If you do not have a veneer press, use adequate hand clamps, pieces of cardboard approximately one-sixteenth-inch thick on each outside surface, and, finally, three-quarter- or one-inch chipboard as stiffener. Keep the work true, flat, and neat. After unclamping, allow all glued-up surfaces at least another day to settle. Work the parts fair, make edge gluings, and only then polish with your finest plane and, if need be, a cabinet scraper.

Veneering opens possibilities. You can use a great deal of fantasy. Once you have learned certain dos and don'ts, there is a freedom in working with veneer that you cannot always achieve with solid wood exclusively. But there is also a good deal of hard, exacting, disciplined work. *Veneering is not a shortcut.* It is really another way of doing certain cabinetmaking. You have to learn the discipline before you can enjoy the freedom of this technique.

Freedom and discipline—we do talk about these things. It is in the times, I suppose, to pit the one against the other, or at least to separate them. Another mode of thinking is that one must be bought at the price of the other: Either we accept discipline and are bound (hampered) by it or we find our own way by first being free to do so. Knowhow is often associated with conservatism; whole groups have rebelled against it, refurnishing a school, so to speak, their way. And much knowledge has been obscured by slogans.

Certainly some teaching is inflexible, gray in its traditionalism, and often as a result of the person or persons involved. But skill is part practice. And practice, if it is to widen experiences, is part discipline. Knowing how to do something well can be binding, yes, if we resign ourselves to method

Making sides of showcase cabinet: Sawn (doussie) veneer, cross-bonded solid core with edge-gluing put on before both surfaces are veneered.

Close-up of top and bottom pieces of same showcase cabinet show how ⅛" cross-bond itself is scored with half-round file before edge pieces are applied. This is to counteract tendency of the soft wood (abaci or sapele) to fuzz, thereby hindering a tight fit.

Clamping mitered edge-gluings with help of specially made angled pressure-block.

alone. Yet more and more we modern creative individuals are admitting that if we are to express what we want to we have to be able to *do* it. With the right spirit, skill is the true beginning of freedom.

Those of us who want to believe in what we do should not turn to veneer unless we have these things clear in our minds. A piece built upon the principle of veneer only is neither better nor worse than one made of solid wood throughout. It is different. And, I hope, different in the better sense of that word. Freedom helps us past some difficult problems of construction, but it brings with it other problems almost as difficult. Freedom without purpose is not enough; we should know why we want to use any particular technique before trying it.

One last word—it could be a slogan for some of us: Veneer as veneer, solid wood as solid wood, and nothing in between.

Side and bottom of case, both veneered, will be doweled together. Shown here with rabbet for frame and panel.

Another construction involving sawn veneer: The side of the music stand is about 7″ wide, has tenon and heel sawn from the same bonded core that forms the base for veneer. Such a wide joint would be inadvisable if the piece were not cross-bonded and, thus, stable.

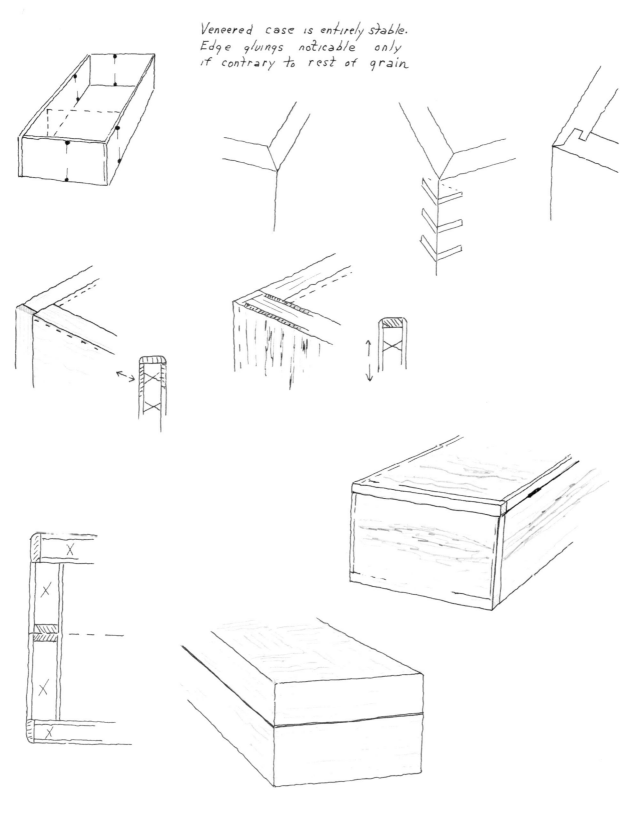

Veneered case is entirely stable.
Edge gluings noticable only
if contrary to rest of grain

Box or case entirely veneered.
Edge gluings "visible" or hidden.
Free choice of grain direction.

45

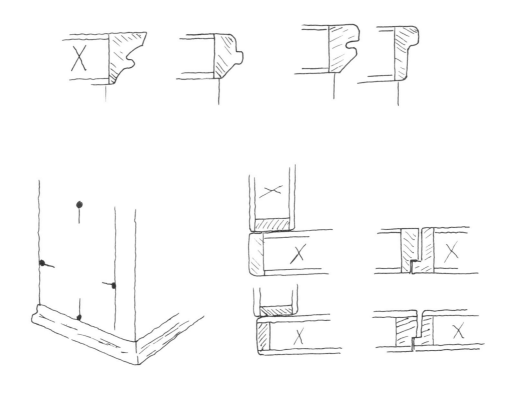

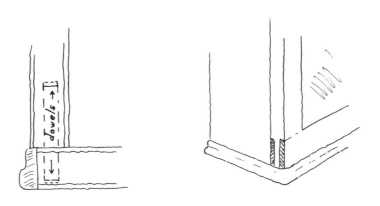

Veneered case (sides, top & bottom) is stable;
can have veneered or frame-panel door and (or) back.
Ample edge gluings (mitred) allow for wide choice
of suitable "moulding" shapes & shadings...
Veneered doors can be discreet, soft-edged.

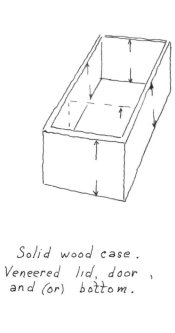

Veneered surface stable

solid wood moves

NO!

Solid wood case.
Veneered lid, door,
and (or) bottom.

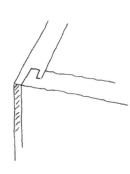

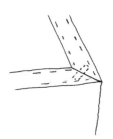

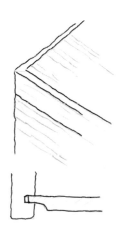

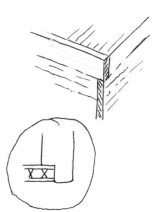

Logic

The term *wood-butcher* is tossed around among us. I guess we've all used it now and then. Probably the meaning of it varies depending on whether one is referring to oneself or to someone else. Nonetheless, a wood-butcher, basically, is a fellow for whom things go wrong. That's one way of looking at it. Another is that the wood-butcher is simply a rough-cut outsider, going his own way, doing odd things, and not really giving a hoot about how one is supposed to do it.

Sometimes our wood-butcher accomplishes rather startling results—for better or for worse. Often it is for worse. After all, the term does have a derogatory implication. I wonder though—it means mistakes, but mistakes by what measure? According to whom? Are they mistakes only when compared to a "this-is-how-one-does-it" scale? Or are they mistakes made consciously, or even unconsciously, because of some conflict with one's own inner self? There is something deep inside most of us that often wants to sort things out before beginning the doing. It wants to know the *why* before the *how*.

Usually, most of us are too late asking the questions; they come in retrospect, and then using the term *wood-butcher* is a good way to sum up the situation. But could it be that the thing that caused us to make the mistakes, that diverted us from the "this is how," is the very thing that might have led

us to our own solution, our own methods, and finally a result—however odd—that suited us better? I suppose if you're an easygoing person living out in the country and about to build a house in the woods, you can just sort of let go, relax, and live the whole experience. There will be a long period of time, and things will simply happen, and the house will grow. Slowly, perhaps disorderly, but it will take shape.

With most (though not all) cabinetmakers it is different. In the making of furniture, mistakes occur much more quickly and are, in a sense, more difficult to correct. There is less leeway in furniture than with a ramshackle house. There's got to be method in the way you work, we say. We like to be emphatic about this. But as I think of it, subjectively now, method is only part of what a good craftsman needs. Logic should come first—at least to some of us. I'm probably rather backward about these things, but for me logic is primary. And it isn't the logic of *process* or *method*. The thing that comes first to me is a sort of feeling down inside, which I suppose is the logic of *purpose*. At least at the beginning, this is so. Later on, another branch of that logic may lead me into method; but first I have a need to determine the meaning of what I am about to do, or attempt to do. I suppose that first logic is connected to the place inside where we sort matters and take a first deep breath. We have to feel good about what we are embarking on; even if it's the start of a long, difficult job of various definite processes we still have to feel good inside, there has to be something central about the whole thing that adds up for us.

For some of us it's logic first and method afterward. Though in teaching it's apt to be the other way around. "Learn the method first," we say. "You'll see the logic of it later on." By and large, this approach works, and I think one of the reasons that it works is that it is not so very often questioned. Sooner or later, however, we encounter the student, a certain type of person really, for whom questioning comes naturally, and then things suddenly become more complex. Logic and method are in a chicken-and-egg relationship. And though we've never sorted out that conundrum, we must, in the case of logic and method, get things fairly right.

I think that if you get that "way-inside thing" straightened out and arrive at the point where you want the experience, sense its meaning, and feel that it will be worth the effort, then you will not really be at odds with yourself. You'll think more clearly. You won't reject methods simply because they are based on other people's experiences. Many of these experiences are worth acquiring; we should accept them and be grateful. There is a certain kind of person who is flexible even about this: He accepts the need for method, for certain ways of doing certain things, and yet makes his own adaptations and interpretations. And he does it all without being at odds with himself.

So your way of going about doing things will be an interpretation of something basically sound. It won't be against the laws of wood, for instance, or of clean work, or the simple truth of good and bad joints, but it will be a series of personal adaptations. It will be yours, with a flexibility and a final clarity of your own. *Even your mistakes will be personal.* And I think personal mistakes are, if I may say so, less painful and more enriching than mistakes made through other people's methods or other people's

measures. One person will say, "I made all these mistakes, this and that is wrong, that's not the way you're supposed to do it." Another might say, "I made these mistakes, that isn't the way I really wanted to do it, I didn't really mean to do this—it just happened." And maybe it just happened because the source of energy for the doing came from outside that person's inner self, outside that place where things are first sorted out.

Crude idea-sketches of cabinet in English brown oak. Panels were first intended to be in ash, slightly convex, with the curve of the grain forming a slit. After four days' work on these, I discarded them.

I'm thinking again of our wood-butcher. Someone wrote a little article on the subject. It was very personal and full of self-irony, a really charming little piece. And, as I recall it, the writer received a lot of messages that said, in effect, "Well, speak for yourself. I hope you don't mean *me*." Does it really matter whom he meant? It's the situation that is interesting, and we all recognize it with its clumsiness, haste, anxiety, and distractions, and that feeling in the end about what "might have been."

Cabinet in brown oak: Searching for proportions of doors with the help of mock-up that includes one sidepiece.

I don't think there is any good reason for denying the fact that most of us have experienced that sort of disappointment. Nor do I look back on these instances as being especially painful or tragic or something not to be talked about. I think that that kind of experience simply belongs to a way of learning for certain people. Maybe the learning goes against some people's grain, which causes this squeaking and sparks in their work.

There are different kinds of craftsmen just as there are different kinds of people. In essence, I suppose, there are the practical ones and the dreamers. And the distance between them is not only ambition, but also a state of being. One person calls himself a wood-butcher because his methods are not efficient enough and he is losing time, and time is money. Another person admits himself to be a wood-butcher because somehow his feelings have become derailed and things have gone wrong, not in relation to time and money, but in relation to something that is, for him, even more important. Maybe this outsider or dreamer craftsman is what we call too poor to be miserly: He can afford to dream.

It occurs to me that the center of all this, the difference between one way and another, is a generosity, a kind of caring. As long as we have a feeling that comes from our core and lends a bit of warmth to what we do and touches the people that our doing brings us in contact with, then those of us who at times can be called wood-butchers are doing rather well, really. Our frustrations are a sign of sincerity and the fact that we want to do better next time. We probably will. And there is no doubt that a bit of humor in the situation of the present will help us to do better in the future.

OPPOSITE: *Cabinet of English brown oak, panels of American spalted maple. Height of case 57cm, total height 139cm, depth 20cm. Wax finish. 1977.*

FOLLOWING PAGES: *The drawers are of Swedish ash with a delicate texture. For the doors, the joints were made with all the members the same thickness. Later, the vertical parts were planed thinner, resulting in a shading that accentuates the horizontal lines of the cabinet.*

We do dwell on the reasons for making mistakes. True, some of those mistakes result simply from not having followed a certain method, or methods. But other mistakes, for another kind of craftsman, are caused by not having followed his "deep-inside" feeling. There is a great difference between the one and the other, just as there is a difference between the people involved. Maybe we could think about this when we look at our own work, or that of others. When we see a nice thing, whether we've done it ourselves or someone else has, and the piece has an appeal, which makes us want to get close to it, then probably there is something special about those shapes. And by shapes I don't mean obvious sweeps and original lines, but small details and proportions. We realize that all this is the result of a way of working and being. It has been said that fine architecture isn't done, it is experienced, or lived. True. The best work we do is really the result of a total experience. It's the way we are, with or without luck.

Certain shapes are a result of a way of working; you cannot divorce the shapes with their details from the process of work itself. And if the process has been a personal adventure for the doer, then it is there in the piece—still a personal experience. All the things we are must be in our work. The difference in our work will be the difference between us as craftsmen. There will be a certain stiffness about the work of those who rely mostly on techniques and want predetermined results; it is almost a rule that stiffness in method leads to stiffness in result. Whereas methods that are our own improvisation on certain logical ways will lead us to other and more personal results, however quaint. And then it doesn't matter what we call ourselves—wood-butchers or something else.

Detail of corner, the brown oak cabinet.

Laminated "bird's-foot," which emerged in the first idea-sketch. It is slightly tapered at each end.

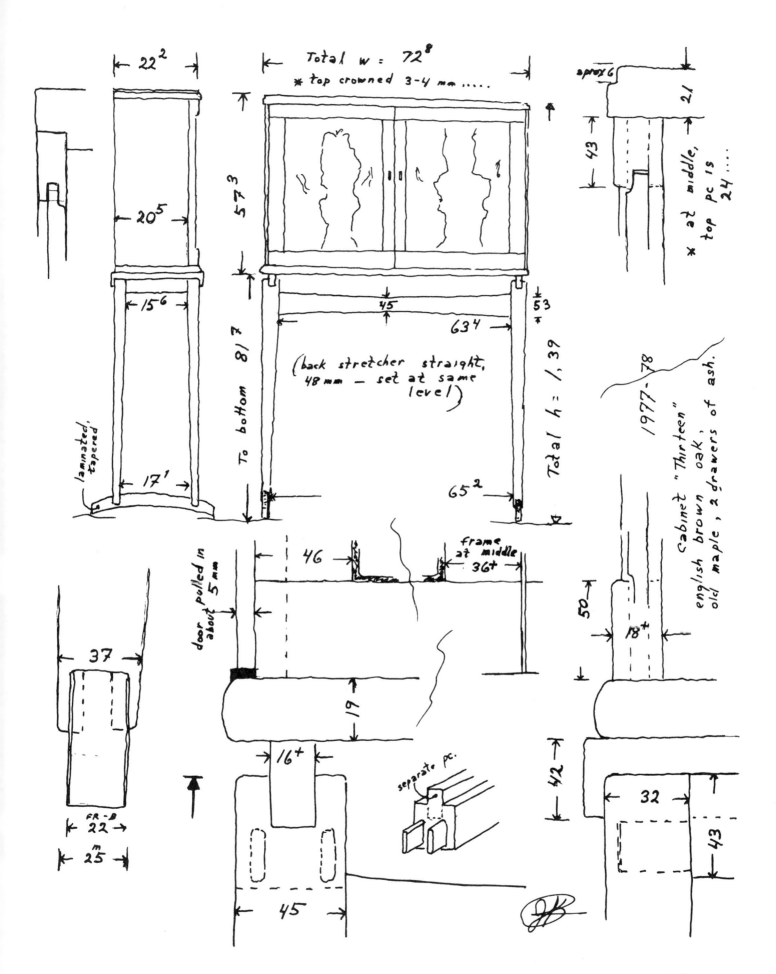

22²

Total w : 72⁸
* top crowned 3-4 mm .....

aprox 6

21

43

* at middle,
top pc is
24 .....

20⁵

57³

15⁶

laminated, tapered

17¹

To bottom 8/7

45

63⁴

53

(back stretcher straight,
48 mm — set at same
level)

Total h : 1,39

65²

1977-78

english brown oak,
old maple, 2 drawers of ash.

cabinet "Thirteen"

door pulled in about 5 mm

46

frame at middle
36⁺

50

18⁺

37

FR-B
22

m
25

16⁺

19

separate pc.

42

32

45

43

Repairing Mistakes?

There is an old saying: A good cabinet-maker can repair his own mistakes. I'd like to put in there the words *some of*. Because certainly there are mistakes that can and should be repaired; it is equally certain that some mistakes are beyond repair. Or should be.

It's a matter of honest judgment. Although there's no denying that it is also a matter of how we feel about these things. As a rule there are, I believe, primarily two kinds of mistakes: those of the hand and those of the mind. Maybe we have gotten a ways into a piece we thought was going to be very fine only to discover that we are on the wrong path: things are not going as we had hoped, the piece taking shape there before us, instead of looking better and more promising, is losing something along the way. Then maybe we have to stop and admit that here is a bad mistake. It is not a technical mistake, a fault in the work itself. It is worse than that: We are on the wrong road.

Being the sort of person and craftsman I am, I simply cannot continue once I see that I am faltering and fumbling in the work. This is not a matter of some high-class principles; it's just that I do not have the energy to continue. Consequently, I have to make a decision: Is there anything that I can save here, parts of this piece I can still redo, or should I just forget it and begin all over again? This is a situation with which many of us amateurs are faced now and

then. The way we decide (on an amateur basis) will depend upon our own personalities.

In a commercial situation I imagine that some craftsmen simply must argue themselves past a point of doubt. They may look at something and realize inwardly that it is not as good as they had hoped, but then a debate takes place inside somewhere and a rationalizing voice is heard to say, "It can yet be made better. You can change this or that. People won't notice these details. . . ." Then comes a seductive whisper, "Maybe it's going to be *even better* that way!" And one continues with the work.

I won't pass judgment on such situations and decisions. They can be a matter of survival for a craftsman who is pressed in a commercial swirl and has to live with various compromises.

Not long ago someone wrote from far away to ask me, "Should I make compromises? If so, what sort of compromises?" I read and reread the letter, realizing there wasn't much I could say to my friend. I ended up by simply suggesting that he try to keep this problem secondary. Let the work have primary importance, let it answer the question. Don't allow the matter of compromise to become more important than the work. This means that the way you work, the things you do and how you do them, your shop, the way you live are in some sort of accord within yourself. You develop a way of living, and if that conflicts with commercial interest, then you must sort it out. Either you adapt your work to commerce or you solve your money problems another way and keep your work what it should be for you. As I've said to myself many times before: Try to live the way you are, be the person in your work that you are in the rest of your life. Easy to say!

To return to repairing mistakes: Aside from getting on the wrong road, there are the "small" everyday things that happen—little accidents, such as a dent or a scratch or a fit that is not altogether what you want it to be. For me, as for any other craftsman, there is a certain satisfaction in being able to see clearly and judge whether or not one of these lesser mistakes can be repaired. Some of them certainly can and should be. All the same, I don't believe in this business of mixing glue and sawdust, or using stain, or the various other rescue methods commonly advertised or recommended among craftsmen, who "have been at it for fifty years."

With repairing mistakes—as with almost anything else we do—there is a crude way and a fine way of going about it. By allowing ourselves to be crude in moments like this—little moments of crisis—we just might develop habits that will spread that crudeness into other parts of our work.

I remember an incident years ago at cabinetmakers' school. There was a young fellow, a good cabinetmaker-to-be, who was near the end of his education; he was doing a very important piece in rosewood and was just a few days from completing it. Well, the fellow was sanding the top of the cabinet, which was veneered, when he sanded through the veneer. The patch where he had done so was hardly noticeable, but it was there; when you turned the light on and looked closely, there it was. Naturally, the fellow was broken up—he simply didn't know what to do.

At the shop we had a resident craftsman, who, though not one of the teachers, was the person to whom we turned at times like this. His name was Arthur. He looked at that piece for a while, muttered, and then went about his other work; he was in the middle of something. The boy kept worrying. He went over to Arthur, and they talked. Arthur went down into the basement where we had our supply of veneer, from which the boy had taken the piece he used in the cabinet. Without saying much, Arthur flicked through the pack of veneer and picked out a piece or two, comparing the pattern he had selected with the wood in the top of the cabinet. He then took a carving chisel—one of those chisels with a half-moon curve—and moved a portable lamp closer to the cabinet where the boy was standing, shaken; one can imagine his feelings, seeing Arthur with chisel poised above his work. Arthur made a single angled cut at each outer edge of the spot that had been sanded through. We all winced. Then he took the piece of veneer he had selected, comparing it once more with the cabinet top. He placed the veneer on his bench, atop a small block, clamped it, and made two cuts. And there was a neat, sharp, oval piece of rosewood veneer. This our master craftsman carefully fitted to the cabinet top. He tested the fit—yes, it was good. He knew that as he glued and pressed this almond-shaped piece into the cabinet top it would fit even more tightly.

Arthur had made what we call a *lus*, a louse. And with it he saved a cabinet. The repair he did was so perfect that when the piece had been polished and finished even we who had seen this repair work done could hardly find the spot. Such is true workmanship.

Maybe for Arthur it was all in a day's work. He had us inexperienced youngsters around him, and similar accidents happened now and then. Was he proud? Perhaps; he smiled, this man of few words. I know that had I been Arthur, I would have been very proud, although I would hardly have worn my pride as modestly as he did.

Marvelous Things

Marvelous things have had their beginning on paper, in sketches and drawings. I know that now, but I learned it too late. Knowing it late leaves me with a twinge of envy. Yet, at the same time and in the same breath, I have to remind myself that many wonderful things have been *lost* on bits of paper. Lost because the person who put them there had his heart elsewhere. For some of us, something good that we are going to do later begins with a premonition. It can come rather quickly, and go just as quickly. And for such people, having to pause and put some of this down on paper—to organize it—dilutes that first feeling. We lose something during the time we're pulling ourselves together and finding the pencil and the paper and rethinking what came to us as but a word, hardly a whisper.

I say this as a very subjective reaction. I know that there are people who need an organization from the beginning. Besides, that inspiration or first feeling of an idea may later on turn out to be quite unrealistic. The way some of us use our habits to keep the idea real and feasible varies, but that's the main point, anyway: From the moment we get an idea and a feeling, we do take different paths. I'm not so sure we have a choice; maybe what directs us is the way we are put together. Some of us, held by habit or by echoes of our education, miss the discoveries that lead to the most important thing of all: the elusive feeling that gave us the first impulse and also helps us to see our way from there.

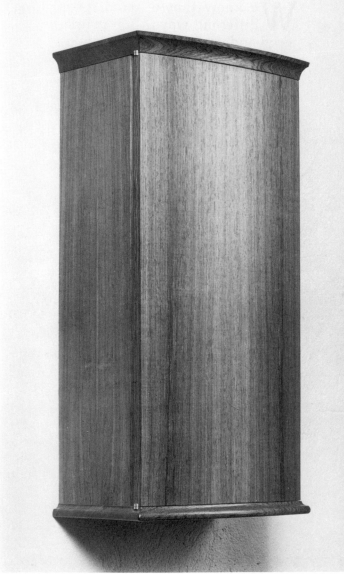

Cabinet of Rio rosewood. Height about 58cm, width 28cm, depth 15cm. Untreated. 1972.

Composing - Another Approach to Design

We know that different people see in different ways. But in the realm of wood and one's work, how does one *learn* to see? More precisely, in making furniture, how can one predict the outcome, how can one be sure his intentions will be realized in the finished piece?

Most courses in woodworking and furniture design include a good deal of drawing: mechanical and perspective drawing, sketching, and so forth. And they are apt to require many hours of what might be called exercises in visual development. Usually these consist mostly in working with shapes and colors and various materials. A lot of very precise drawing—with various geometrical solutions and proportions, perspective views, and also some measured exercises— goes along with this regimen. I'm not at odds with this in the broad sense, because I think that a large number of those attending such courses are generally satisfied. Certainly, most of them do get something out of it; they feel that it is positive, stimulating, maybe even exciting. At the same time, there are always those for whom this is interesting, yes, but also rather confusing.

I remember visiting a school in Canada where students would come back from a session of design exercises with their notebooks packed full—ten to fifteen pages—of all kinds of drawings: ideas they had, things to be made in wood, tremendously stimulating imagery—on paper. They'd come to one of the teachers with these; there would be a little discussion. And, more often than not, going into the possibilities and discussing the idea on the basis of work in wood, they would discover that all these sketches, wild ideas conceived in an atmosphere of purely visual stimuli, led to uncertainty and frustration. These were images without the feel of wood, or ideas in which the material was neutralized; there wasn't enough consideration given to the properties of the material to be used. These exercises, finally, took the students *away from* the possibilities of wood and their ability to work in tune with it. They wouldn't believe the first person who suggested this and warned them about the obstacles; they'd go to another teacher. All the same, there was no getting around the fact. Anyone who knew and cared about wood as a material would perceive the central problem and ask, "Can this be done in wood?" Sometimes all concerned would admit that it could not; other times, it had to be tested and proved, the hard way.

The fundamental fault of such an approach, which urges us to start with "originality," is that trying to adapt the idea to wood will cause the idea to isolate itself. In a sense, it will be too strong for the wood, because its demands on the wood cannot be met without a misuse of wood. The result is disappointment of one sort or another.

What occurs often with a very original idea that is visually aimed and is based upon intricate patterns or uninhibited sculptural forms that work on paper—"talking about rather than working with"—is that even if the concept can be carried through in wood, the student-cabinetmaker himself is not skilled enough to do so. The various courses in drawing, these visual exercises in geometric juggling and so forth, take a great deal of time, and the students do not have enough chance to develop the skills with which they could carry through even some of the less impossible ideas.

The school, you see, was supposed to produce both craftsmen and designers (and, being government subsidized, it was to turn out useful citizens). No doubt because of this double aim, it produced something in between. This is all too often true. Education aimed at achieving that complete product, the designer-craftsman, will fall short of both. The fact is, there ain't no such animal, except on paper. True, fine crafts do include design, but only as an integral part of the craft process itself; it belongs to wholeness in a given craft. When a would-be craftsman starts out with design as a mainspring, we get design, yes, but also contrived, artificial craft. When a designer sticks to design, we're apt to get good design as such, useful if we use it in the right way. When a fine craftsman sets about doing his work and does it with that purpose only, as craftsmanship, we get good craft that is also good design—but it is good design in retrospect, as a result of its first being good craftsmanship. When does craft become art? I do not know. Unless, maybe, also only after the fact, because essentially it is, first and foremost, fine craft.

In the practical sense of the term, *design* has undergone a fundamental change during recent years. We had once a cooperative effort between a designer and, let us say, a craftsman or cabinetmaker; they got together and developed a prototype, giving consideration to the requirements and limitations of certain manufacturing techniques, and later offered this to a production unit, to industry, large or small. For a while it worked, especially in Scandinavia. But at the present time the impressiveness of coupling design achievement with the work of a purely professional craftsman has worn thin. As of late woodcraft in Europe has deteriorated. Even in a country like Denmark things are nearly at a standstill. I will be contradicted on this, but I believe it; as far as the future craftsman in wood is concerned, in the personal sense of craft, this is true. For nearly three decades the Danes were foremost in producing excellent furniture, the best of its kind. Theirs was an achievement belonging to a period when a new concept of furniture was clarified. The talented architect designed functional, clean-lined, truly good-looking furniture. The cabinetmaker developed, together with technicians, the means to produce these often intricate pieces in a way that included respect for the material and a good deal of traditional know-how. But, and I say it regretfully, with a minimum of handwork. This was a team effort, yes; nonetheless, it was the designer who was most evident as a *person*. The cabinetmaker was rather anonymous; his role was more that of a technician, a professional workman, than of a craftsman. One of the designs could be executed by five or six such cabinetmakers and even in broad daylight most of us could not tell who had made which. There were no cabinetmaker's fingerprints on the work. Maybe there were not supposed to be, although such products were—and still are—presented as something special and the cabinetmaker named as a master, his name adding to the prestige (and price) of the piece. There was an air of the extraordinary about it all, which was justified at that time and on that particular technical level.

Such furniture is, let's admit it, production work in the true sense, and it could be made just as well in larger quantities. After all, once we get together the design, the jigs, the machines, and the skill, we can produce fine things in quantity—if we want to. It is simply that in our time we are, as a rule, not concerned enough to do so. Or we deliberately avoid, as with cars and a lot of other items, doing things as well as they could be done.

So now we have Danish fine furniture—still fine, but in trouble. Some of the exclusiveness is hard to defend, especially as regards price. Is this, after all, handcrafted furniture? Is it unique enough to merit the high cost? For some pieces, yes; it is better than most of what is being marketed. But this is by no means always or even often the case. Furthermore, very few new designs have emerged during the past decade. Honestly now, for how long can one be clearly original in a particular and somewhat limited field as this, using only one material: wood? Maybe it is the end of an epoch.

We are faced now with a polarization, which requires that a choice be made: either the mass-produced object of varying quality, including the highest; or, in sharp contrast to the marketed product, the truly unique handmade piece with the cabinetmaker's fingerprints on it. In the second case, it is not only the design, but also the process itself that has its message, the cabinetmaker's personal mark. It is a real dilemma, but before we can solve it we will first have to admit that there is a dilemma. And there is a reluctance to do that. Then there will be the need for a new and better crafts education, which teaches a more personalized workmanship with an intimate relationship to materials—fingertip skills. In other words, the wholeness of the creative process must be rediscovered and taught. This will mean less emphasis on design as such and more attention to the craftsman who, if he excels, will also produce things that are fine design, but that will be such as result more than as an intention.

As yet there is no sign of such rethinking. After a golden era looms a very uncertain future. A few people believe that by encouraging craftsmen to more personal methods and a certain degree of independence one advocates tearing down the old, disregarding tradition and thoroughness. No so! The essential soundness of the craft must be preserved. The rightness that has developed in the course of generations of working with a particular material is as usable today as it ever was. If, however, a new generation of rather independent young people are going to become craftsmen, they want to feel that the past is not the terminus, the final limitation of their craft, but rather a good beginning on which to build something as sound, yet more personal. Unless some people can see the reality of this, nothing can keep alive—much less renew—what has been at the center of what was best about Danish furniture.

It is possible to imagine an ideal sort of situation: a good designer teamed with a good craftsman, who could do his own interpretation of the designer's intention—two creative personalities, both present in the final small-scale product. So far as I can see, the material odds are against such ventures, although there are, in America, attempts being made. We can hope that, in that more open climate, these will succeed, if only for a while.

Let's return to education and the realities it must face regarding the designer-craftsman. Already at the design stage the emphasis has changed to what one might term the "sellable." One begins from the market end of the problem: What do people want? What do young people, let us say (who are a large percentage of the buying public), look for in the way of furniture? Make a research of this and determine the need, and then fill the need with a team of designers. The designers work together, but they are now independent of cabinetmakers. These designers go directly to the industry, to the machines that will be working, to the production methods. They are less concerned than were their small-scale predecessors with sensitivity or quality or aesthetics in the lasting sense of those words. They want a temporary product to fill a temporary need. And that will be made in a very efficient way. With that aim they do exciting and interesting things, but they go about it in a purely commercial, calculated way.

They must have an extremely thorough knowledge of many sorts of material, the various techniques, the costs, and the salability of the end product. They must follow production trends and public tastes and methods of marketing. It becomes, in other words, a design industry rather than a designer here and a designer there working with a cabinetmaker and applying certain considerations to fine woods and good taste. We cannot toss around the word *designer* as we used to.

Now, if a school is to produce a designer who will survive in the field, it has to be equipped to do so. A few schools are. But the way of doing this is distinctly different from what it takes to turn out a good craftsman. The craftsman has to produce noticeably personal things through his very own skill. His fantasy and methods become good design *only* when he is a truly fine craftsman. Not before that. Whereas the designer, whether or not he has once been a craftsman or would like some day to be one, is more or less divorced from the craftsman's way of living and working.

A certain kind of craftsman—a kind of person, really—is apt to be unsatisfied with what a school can provide. One learns techniques—drawing, layout—a bit about design, yet somehow the approach is geared to a generalized concept of what a craftsman should be. There is nothing wrong with this except that it provides most for those who fit the pattern, for whom methods—drawing, selection of wood, the techniques themselves—are very predictable, as efficient as possible, and as free as possible from risks of any kind. There is often an element of speculation in this: Craft education wants to present itself as a good investment, as being risk-free.

I think one of the things that is apt to be regarded as a risk is the questioning by some students of the validity of this approach. True, the majority of students want things to be predictable, they want to draw well or try to do so, and they believe they can convey their intentions on a piece of paper

or a working drawing and follow that and arrive at a desired result. Many can, and for those this is the right way of going about it.

But—and it is an irritating *but*—there are always those for whom this is unsatisfying. They are unsure from the beginning. There is something in their very nature that is in conflict with this sureness. Again I am reminded that there are basically two different types of craftsman: the one who wants to be sure and for whom work is method and efficiency and predictable results; and the one who is the outsider, the person for whom there must always be an element of adventure, which is closely connected with uncertainty. For this craftsman the most-used road leads to a fence.

We are back again to the question of how one learns to see and to develop methods that will fit one's own nature and needs.

It is not unusual for people who have studied form and design to be able to draw in a way that gives them early self-assurance. They sketch well, they know about layout, and they work from that point for a while after they have finished school . . . only to find it is not altogether right for them. Gradually, some of them learn more about their material. They leave paper and go more into the wood. Late in their cabinetmaking or woodworking life they discover the whole of it for themselves: their own method of going about building a piece of furniture. The word I choose to describe this process of weaving together material and methods is *composing*. To put it simply: There are those who draw their way to things and those who build (or compose) their way to them.

Drawing usually confuses me, probably because I'm bad at it. So it's a natural thing for me to compose my pieces rather than draw them. And I can share a few experiences along this line, for whatever they are worth. Suppose we get an idea for a piece of furniture. Maybe it begins with a function—the piece is directed toward usability—with perhaps shapes and details that are second-

Music stand, natural pearwood. Height with rack
folded about 68cm. Waxed. 1977.

ary. Or perhaps it's the other way around; we have a need for shapes and proportions, an object we feel would be visually enjoyable and it may or may not fill a function. Early on, perhaps from the very start, we link this to the material. For some it's like the chicken and the egg—who knows which came first, the idea or the material? It's really unimportant which came first, but it is nice when they come together. So we make some rough sketches, or maybe we don't. That is less important than that we have the urge to go on.

And I think that it is at this stage—before we have gotten into the work, while we're standing there with the wood and thinking of what we want to do and some of the methods that will be involved in doing it—that we begin almost subconsciously to sort

things out in our minds. What is at the very center of wanting to do a piece? From where will the energy come? It can be doing the work itself that matters to us. The result, which we hope will be pleasing, is not central; it's the fact and feel of work that are. Or it may be the usability of the finished object combined with its final appeal. In either case, we regard the methods, the difficulties, the probable enjoyments. The unpredictable is there, too; something, an element of uncertainty, pulls us like a magnet. We weigh the risks. What is the most "dangerous" part of the work? The most critical stage of it? Is it the beginning or something further on? Sort it out. At first it takes time, later it becomes easier. Anxiety is natural here, but fear is not an ally; we must overcome it in order to think clearly—in our own way.

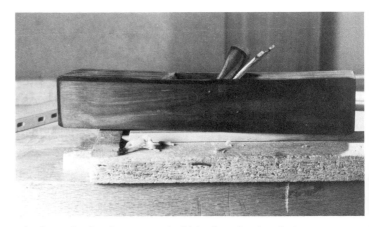

Block with glued-on stop, held in bench vise, helps when hand-planing the fifty or more slats.

Marking for mortises in frame to take tenons on slats. Any slight variation on template is repeated. The result: Although space between one row and the next is not identical, the slats remain aligned.

Slats showing tenon: Since these are not glued, each must fit its mortise exactly.

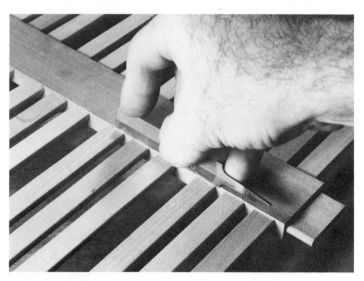

Slats, underside rounded inward to lessen visual sense of thickness.

Topside of frame with slats: A "line" is carefully scored with a saw file.

Gluing-up frame: Note that the frame is lifted by cross-pieces level with screw-on clamp. This gives a straight-on pressure and allows easier access for clamping blocks (faced with tape so they will not stick) at each corner. Only the frame parts are glued, the slats simply fit snugly in their respective mortises. The midsection of the frame, with its tenon, slips into a mortise made a trifle too wide, thus equalizing the distance between the two sections.

Some of us tend to reshuffle methods and do things, if not backwards, then at least sideways, devoting the most attention and care to making that part of the object that involves the greatest effort and the most uncertainty, saying to ourselves that if we get past this the rest will not be so difficult. These sideways methods or unorthodox procedures may seem quaint to some professionals and may be ridiculed in some circles. But they do serve a certain kind of person very well. And that is what matters.

In fact, there is meaning in this apparent lack of order. At the very center of composing are three things: curiosity, uncer-

The music stand: Frame-and-panel surface with notched pieces into which rack fits for the various positions. With rack raised, the stand accommodates a standard score (partiture).

tainty, and energy. One knows there are steps here that cannot be predicted. One feels a richness and a promise in the work that may exceed one's expectations. And one tries to observe what happens as one goes along. I think this last is very important. You have to be able to be your own teacher when you do this sort of composing. Learn from each and every experience. At each step, look, back up, and look again. Change things around, reshuffle some parts, turn a piece upside down, lengthen or shorten it in order to look at it in another perspective, and so on. All these things should interest you. They contribute to your education—or, for some of us, self-education.

You may have noticed that I keep harping on my pet theme: We need to observe ourselves as we work, not just to look at what we are doing, but to see what is happening, where the work is taking us, because if we cannot observe and really notice what is taking place, how will we ever see the connection between what we are doing and where it is leading us?

I have touched upon the graphics of wood: grain pattern and oddities of color. When it comes to developing ways of composing pieces, we need to be aware of another factor, namely, the weight experience of a particular wood. Each wood lends its own feel to a piece of furniture; the way we experience it is related to shape, size, and something I can describe only vaguely as weight. Consistency. Proportion changes with it. So does the feeling of shapes. In one wood a particular shape is relaxed; in another, this same shape is tense, it now has greater density, a different feel. A different sound, too. Not being truly aware of this is perhaps one reason why many of us turn to exaggerated forms and coarse dimensions. These are exciting, we say. True. But for others they are banal, even distracting.

These days, taste—what we like and dislike—seems to be widely divergent. One person might seriously claim that aesthetics is merely a matter of opinion; there are no reliable measures, he will say. A sculptor reminds us that natural forms are rich and varied, and his shapes, derived from natural forms and then metamorphosed into art, share that rich variety. Whereas a box is a box, he claims; it is experienced at a glance, and that is all there is to it. This strikes me as a rather immature statement. Besides, when it comes to shapes, nature's originals are usually the best.

As long as it feels right and you enjoy it, you should believe in what you are doing. Don't let yourself be sidetracked by doubtful onlookers, people who say, "That's not exciting. You don't know where you're going with all those pick-and-poke details. You're wasting your time." At such moments, know yourself, remember that you feel good working this way. Maybe then it's a nice way to "waste" time. . . .

From the very start, look for more than meets the eye. Discover details, even if the discovery seems to be by chance. They will lead you to others. Gradually the difference between one way of doing things and another will emerge as what it really is: the difference between one craftsman and another. For this composing we need an open mind and wide-open, observing eyes. We have to regard a measure of uncertainty as being a natural part of the process as we make changes at various steps of the work, observe the effects, and yet remain aware of the details that can be added to enhance the effect of each possibility. Our sensitivity we can develop, but from early on we must trust in patience. *To live with our uncertainty we need patience.* For the right person this approach will work. Experience is like a snowball—it keeps building on itself.

The ways of beginning a piece no doubt vary with the kind of piece it is, and, of course, with the person who is going to do the work. At times we simply have a bit of wood. Fine wood, probably a small piece of it. And we say to ourselves, "That is lovely; I must make something out of it." And because we have so little it is going to be a small object—a carved box or something of the sort. With that wood as an impulse, we go ahead. The procedure and the source of impulse or inspiration will vary. A table probably begins with a combination of purpose, shapes, and wood, wood that may or may not be really precious, but should be the kind out of which you can make a good table, and give it a proper finish. Likewise a chair: We may have a practical idea for a chair or we may want to be original and twist a simple idea into a fantasy chair.

With a chair there may be sketches and, very likely, working drawings, because a chair is a complicated structure. One needs to think it through, beginning with the basic problems of the height at which one sits, the angle, the position and shape of the backrest. There is a great deal of predetermining, requiring a combination of the visual and the practical. We are apt to make and follow a drawing. That brings us closer to being designers, because now we begin to get into the matter of predictability, staking everything on the fact that we have drawn a chair that is worth doing and will be the way we want it to be. This is a departure from the composing technique as such, but it's a concession that some of us may have to make at times. Or may even *want* to make.

With a cabinet, the approach is still different. I think it is more vague than with a chair. And there is more involvement with color, surfaces, and proportions.

Some craftsmen like to make models before doing a piece that is fairly complex and involves a great deal of time and work. Models can be made out of wood similar in color and mood to what one will be looking for in the piece itself. Or they can be models simply for the sake of a basic proportion or shape or a balance of components. Then one can make them in plasticine, as some sculptors do, or of balsa wood or even cardboard. If we make models in wood and they are models of fairly involved furniture such as chairs, fancy tables, or certain cabinets, then the model itself becomes a project. There is nothing wrong with this; making

models is very enjoyable. I did it for a year or two in connection with some work I was doing with an architect friend. And I learned something from those models. For me, the memory of that experience is still the pleasure of making models. Being a meticulous person, I made neat models—on a scale of one to five, or sometimes even one to ten—of chairs and other things intended for restaurants and public places. I don't know whether the architect got all that much information from the models. He liked them, they were pleasant to look at, but whether or not they were really the basis for the working drawing, in detail, only he can say.

One risk is that the models themselves tend to have a deceptive appeal because they are often fine-lined and look delicate. Everything is so pleasantly concentrated in a model. It takes a good deal of experience and judgment to be able to predict how the finished piece itself will look—in what ways it will differ from the model. So I think there is an element of wishful thinking in models when they are well made. And perhaps there is a vagueness in models that are just thrown together to, as we say, "get the idea of the thing." Finding the right starting point is a personal matter; you can try models and see where it leads.

It's the same with sketching. A few crude lines may be enough for one craftsman; another may need something more complete and promising in the way of a sketch. For one person a drawing solves problems, it is reassuring. I believe those who rely on drawing are generally less aware of certain factors, such as the way a shape or proportion will be affected by the color and pattern of the wood itself, how a curve or edge or surface will catch light, or feel as we touch it. Maybe they care less about these things than does the other fellow, or somehow believe they can "work it all out" beforehand. They have the impression that if the design is good, the piece will be good. And this is enough. For them the work itself, then, is like following a certain path that leads to a certain place, as quickly as possible.

For another craftsman drawing poses more problems than it solves. There is so much he cannot see or predict on paper—things that have to be brought out directly by the work. His awareness of these "somethings" makes drawing a distraction. The search that is so important is not just for the sake of searching, or as an escape from the discipline drawing implies. He is quite capable of discipline; it's just that he wants discipline, too, as part of another reality. He needs to develop another and more direct way because that is the only way he can perceive what he wants to do and how he should do it.

Sketching or drawing or composing: What works for one person may not work for the next. People see differently; they are different. I suppose that whereas one looks for a *solution* (results), the other is searching for *content* (experiences). The final criteria are the relationship of the person to the sketch or model and the relation, in turn, of that to the way he goes about working.

Whatever the beginning, the main characteristic of the work of composing pieces, in my view, is the fact that, whether from sketch or model, or neither, the final product is the result of a process that involves a step-by-step search. Whether it is mostly method, or intuition and method in some sort of inner balance, the process is in essence a searching as we go along. And the search really should not end until the piece is finished.

My own path to what I call composing was this: At school we did "working" drawings of more or less imaginary pieces, were told the usual things about the usual tools, were sent to museums to do study sketches and measure-ups, and then were required to make furniture not of our own design. Most of us disliked the fact that so much of the course was not, as we looked at it, "for real." Later I did models—pleasant but frustrating—and sketches or bit-drawings that left me tensely on the edge of something. That was when I turned to my fine wood and tools for help. With these I began to build pieces. I've upped the word to *composing*, but to me *building* sounds better even now.

Another symptom of the shortcomings in schools teaching woodworking is that the students themselves, having left and begun to work on their own, recognize that there are a lot of things they should have been taught, but were not. It is sad; they feel cheated. Too many students have not been brought along far enough to develop even the beginnings of independent self-expression. In fact, some of them were—and are—steered away from it. This may be one of the reasons why, both in schools and out, and lately in wide circulation magazines, there is an increasingly large number of exercises in reproduction. The magazines feature articles and drawings and descriptions of "period" furniture, and many craftsmen are doing these reproductions with little deviation from or personal interpretation of the printed words. And this is where my questioning comes in: I am not sure that the reason behind all this duplicating is positive and constructive. Making a "period" piece of furniture—colonial or Shaker or whatever—is an exercise in woodworking. Granted. Following drawings or a working description is learning something. And yet, for the amount of effort involved, there is, I feel, little real creativity. And, for a certain kind of person, there is no personal satisfaction, aside from that of being able to do something in a way that has been predetermined by others.

I wouldn't say no to a student or a friend wanting to do this. Really I would not. But I would ask a few questions first, among them whether it wouldn't be a good idea to use only the mood of a period, person, or piece, and then work freely, following, not drawings, but one's own reaction to the mood itself.

An example of what I mean can be seen if we look at Shaker furniture, not as designs only, but as symbols of a way of living, of a philosophy and religion based on austerity. That austerity is apparent in the workmanship and cleanness of line of the furniture. I believe that the experience, and admiraton, of Shaker furniture is partly emotional and, whether or not some would admit it, it is also aesthetic. It's one of the few clear illustrations of the appeal—ideological, emotional, and aesthetic—of fine proportions and simplicity.

Another example of working from the mood of a period or style, rather than from the literal designs, can be seen in art nouveau furniture. If we look at the work done in the nineteenth and early twentieth centuries, we can be tremendously impressed with the intricacy and imagination—the total achievement—such pieces represent. And I think that it could inspire humility in some of us who are sculpturally inclined and who believe we are working in an exciting and innovative way today.

If we are humble and yet open-minded, we can assimilate impressions from other times and create a mood which will permit us to do something along those lines in the honest light of the feel of the inspiration or the ideas these other people have left us. We're all influenced by someone or something—that's natural. If we could screen out the rigid details, measurements, and such and allow ourselves to be fairly free, not to follow drawings or step-by-step descriptions, but to begin with the idea of wanting to do something in a mood, then we can work as independently as possible and conceive something that is our own, even if it is also an expression of a given theme. I'm not much for second-hand expressions in woodwork; they bring to mind those instances where in theater and music and other arts we allow ourselves to distort in the name of interpreting something that has already been done to completion. Whatever the influence, if we temper our ambition with respect and taste, we will be less apt to distort. I say this with a mixture of hope and doubt, because the temptation to imitate seems to be irresistible, especially when it satisfies the ego, fools the gullible, and fills the pocketbook.

Starting Point

When we are about to do a new piece, or a variation on one done before, some of us need to find a connecting link between our thoughts and the work itself. A few ideas, or inspiration, if you choose to call it such, may hit us like a bolt of lightning. Maybe then we think, "That's great, now I've got it!" But it isn't necessarily true. Any bolt of energy can leave you confused. At such times, some of us need, as the first step into the work itself, to make a connection between idea and method, or even, beyond method, the reality of doing the work. We search and grope for something tangible, and maybe we miss what is right there before us, because it is so close, so ridiculously obvious.

Sometimes this first step can be childishly simple. I once knew a man, a designer, who had been creating furniture for years and years. And yet always, when he was about to begin the design of a chair (or a table or another piece of furniture), he would take a ruler or a tape measure from his pocket and go down on his knees on the floor near the first chair he came across and start measuring it. Usually he'd begin with the height from the floor to the seat. Now, he knew perfectly well this measurement was somewhere between forty-two and forty-five centimeters, roughly eighteen inches. He had done this kind of measuring hundreds, if not thousands, of times before. Likewise, he knew the angle of the back, as he did the width of the seat. All these things were imprinted somewhere deep in his mind. To some of us he cut a ridiculous figure—crawling there on the floor, making these measurements, mumbling to himself, "Yes, yes." It was as if he had suddenly and for the first time discovered that the height to the seat of a good dining chair is forty-four centimeters! This was the way he started his designs. Not always, but very often. And for him, it worked.

Details of same piece.

Showcase cabinet of Tasmanian blackwood. Oil finish. 1977.

FACING PAGE: *The cabinet I call "A Playful Thing."*
Stand is of East Indian rosewood, surfaces of
Andaman padouk. Wax finish. 1977.

Detail of cabinet on facing page: The "roof" with its
supporting parts.

Detail of the chess table.

Music stand of natural pearwood, in open and
closed positions. Wax finish. Wood is from root-end
of a tree, where reddish color can be found free from
cracks, if one is lucky. . . .

The last silver chest. American spalted maple, drawers of bird's-eye maple. Oil finish. 1977.

Detail of silver chest.

English brown oak cabinet on stand, door panels of spalted maple. Wax finish. 1977. Drawers (shown in detail) are of Swedish ash.

A Writing Table

Weird tables, some call them "original" tables, are beyond my reach. Plain ones aren't satisfying enough, taking as they do so much fine wood I cannot quite account for afterwards. A whole big fine plank, eight feet of it—and only a tabletop! In the end, I say to myself, "Having made a table, one is apt to get involved with chairs." Some people claim that if you can make a chair, you can make anything. Could be. But nowadays almost anything can be a chair. As one for whom a chair isn't just anything, I find making a good, simple chair is indeed a frightening challenge. I have yet to gather the courage.

I spent part of one winter at my workbench involved with paper rather than with wood. It was not a comfortable arrangement, with the straight edge of that bench against my ribs—which is perhaps why I became a bit more aware of what a comfortable table for writing might be, for me at least. As I work, the paper twists to the left, my right arm creeps farther onto the table, while my left elbow vainly seeks support. So I thought: a smallish table, curving out toward the left would be nice. The idea makes sense. There would be shapes to work with, and there could be a drawer on the right-hand end, accessible without requiring one to move his chair.

I made a very crude sketch on a piece of chipboard, and it disappeared, no doubt during one of my frenzies of cleaning up. Then one day (I was still writing), I took a large piece of cardboard—the kind used for painting posters—and cut out a rough shape, which I then put aside. Still, for some time, nothing happened; I was into other things. Some time later, I began moving some planks in the machine room where they are stacked against a wall. There I came upon the wood that definitely put me on the track to my table. Several years before, I had nagged my way to a small log of exquisite Italian walnut—the only one in captivity, the wood dealer said. And he charged me accordingly. It had been sawn to two- and two-and-a-half-inch thicknesses. I had a two-inch, near-the-center plank left; there was the wood with the curve I wanted, a curve that originated at my workbench and had taken a further but still vague form on a piece of cardboard. Now it had new meaning, it was in the plank. The piece had a bit of a taper as well (one end came from the base of the tree). It thinned toward the other end, and I saw that along with the curve I would get this taper, which corresponded roughly to the shape of my table. There would be enough wood for the top, and some left over further up for the legs and skirt.

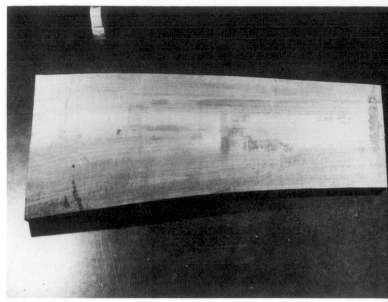

Italian walnut, with curve and taper, pointed the way to a special table, and meant jointing two halves in a line that follows the grain.

What I chose for the top came from the butt end of the log. I got two layers, which were to be put side by side, preserving both taper and curve. But before I could make the cut to get the two equal thicknesses, I had to divide the plank down the middle, with a straight cut there. The other two edges were still curved. I got my thicknesses and laid the pieces side by side. The pattern and the taper were exciting. Yes, this could well be a tabletop worth the wood! But how to join the two halves and yet keep the fine pattern of that curve? If I straightened those two edges to make the usual straight joint, I would lose some of the shape and its colors. In many cases this would not matter so much, but with this table it would definitely be a loss. I did the only thing there was left to do: For the first time, I joined two curved edges. I planed them together with the help of one of my curved planes. And I tell you, I'm not at all sure I want to do that again! It took about a day and a half, and it taught me this: The difference between a very good joint and one that is not quite as good is infinitesimal. The slightest touch of a plane or a file can make that difference. I'd get it almost right, and then maybe take just one little stroke of the plane too much somewhere, and spoil it, and then I'd have to start over again. As I say, I finally did it. Fortunately, I had a good deal of spare width on both pieces. It is satisfying now to look at that surface, with all its curves unbroken; somewhere on it—oh, one can find it if one looks closely enough, but for the sake of vanity let me say "somewhere"—there is a joint.

A word about dowelling. We have all heard at least one person claim that he can always tell when a joint is dowelled because there are cracks and bulges, all sorts of faults along the joint. Like a lot of other statements tossed around, this is only partially true. Most of the things we do can be done right or they can be done wrong. In Europe, the very best cabinetmakers have been using dowels in joinery for a long, long time. With fine, honest results. They do it right. And done right, dowelling, including joining pieces edgewise, is an asset, not a

liability. I will be the first to admit that a perfect joint in wood that is not oily or otherwise extremely difficult to glue should hold without dowels; although with the more cranky woods, like teak, dowels properly used can prevent that first little letting go, which later would spoil the entire joint. But what I wanted to bring up here is something else. Besides its role in strengthening a joint, which may or may not be subject to discussion, there is this to be said about dowelling: It is a way of keeping on the same plane the two parts of a surface being joined; it helps to align the parts of a joint. In this case, the dowels do not necessarily have to also strengthen the joint. We can use very small, short dowels, maybe one-eighth or three-sixteenths of an inch in diameter and only one inch long, and if we place them accurately, these dowels—say five or six along a length of two feet—will guide the two parts exactly in line. Then, when we are alone gluing this important joint, we do not have to have forty-seven clamps and pieces of wood crosswise and do a juggling act. There are a lot of situations where lining up and positioning pieces of wood to be glued can be helped along with small dowels, and this is worth remembering.

The leaf turned out well, strengthening my belief in the idea of the table. The rest of the wood was beautiful, too. One doesn't risk such wood for trial pieces of legs and stretchers. Since I was very uncertain about the final proportions and dimensions of these, I took some pieces of alder and roughly bandsawed three trial legs: one straight, one tapering toward the floor, and one with an upward flare. Here were three very different legs, though, truthfully, I suppose I was already on the way to the solution or shape to which my inclination leads me. I am partial to an upward flaring shape, firmly planted on the floor, but a shape with the chance for many variations. How many variations? Quite a few; at least, more than I dare try. Some of you are refreshingly bold, and do shapes and things just for the heck of it, like doing a somersault in public. Anyway, to confirm my in-

Various stages in composing the idea for a writing table with the help of trial legs and skirts.

ABOVE: *A disturbing detail. This shows the need to flair the skirt at the outside, following the shape of the leg.*

OPPOSITE: *Resulting laminated skirt has outer layer about 8mm thick.*

clination rather than to argue it, I made these three kinds of legs. And yes, the upward flaring one suited me and the table I wanted to do.

By then I was really into the work. I sawed two curved stretchers, or skirts, to the curved shapes of the table leaf. These I propped up under the leaf together with the legs. They were very awkward, but they did point in a definite direction. The clumsiness was a challenge; I had to get past it to find what I hoped for. The upward flaring leg had to be thinner, and the shape, I could see, needed improving. I resawed it, tried it again, and still it was too awkward. At least it seemed awkward when I placed it on the right-hand, or narrower, end of the table. But when I moved it to the outer left-hand corner, an interesting thing happened: Suddenly, it was no longer too heavy! It looked good there. What I hadn't realized, inexperienced as I am with tables, is that such a piece of furniture is not only shapes,

but also a volume, the parts of which have different weights. So this is the way it turned out: The corner of the table where the two curved edges meet has the thickest leg, the left-hand corner at the back edge of the table has the leg that is next largest, and the two legs at the narrower short end of the table are fairly equal to each other, but are smaller than either of the other two. Thus the table has three different size legs. The discovery that led to this was fun, and walking around my table, looking at it from different angles, I find the result makes sense. It is a question of volumes and weights. I really learned something here.

Being excited at that early stage while shaping the legs must have helped me to notice things. I saw that the flared leg was good, but I also noticed that there was a conflict at the point where it joined the vertically placed curve of the skirt. The leg flared while the skirt, or stretcher, was vertical, creating a disturbing shadow. The skirt would have to flare with the legs, which meant that the outer layer of its laminate had to be thick enough to allow me to saw the flare and yet not saw through the outer laminate and into a glued joint.

At first I thought the outside of the curved skirt should be flush with the corresponding part of each leg, that they should nicely flow into each other. As it turned out later, I realized that even if that were so, the leg, with its color, grain, and shape, would cut through the skirt. Better to bring it out a bit from the skirt and accentuate this fact softly by having a rounded edge and a slight shading there. The trial legs had led me to roughly the dimensions I wanted; I made the walnut legs themselves, and the grain pattern of these worked fairly well with the shape. And I thought: Maybe I should do that with the stretchers, too. So I began again studying what was left of my walnut plank and selected pieces for the laminate with the grain running the way I wanted, in a slight dip along the curved (left) end of the table and in an upward sweep along the front curve, where one sits. I sawed the layers with a few extra pieces in case of an

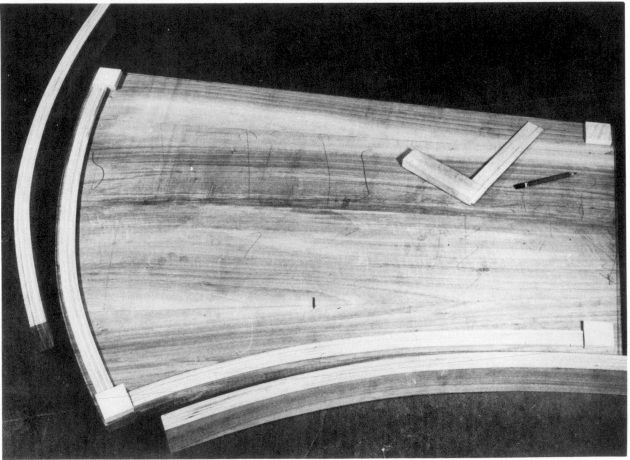

TOP: *Grain and color pattern of skirt are chosen to work with the principal curves of the table.*

BOTTOM: *Laying out with help of thin pieces of laminated skirt parts and cut-off from legs.*

accident, made the form, and did the gluing with the pieces for the skirts slightly wider than they needed to be. From each of these I sawed a piece about one-quarter-inch thick. This helped me very much with the layout: I could get right my various angles for the joints without risking the skirts-to-be. These joints are mortises and spline tenons, done with the accuracy I think the wood deserves. They are strong and neat.

I was as optimistic as I dared be, and was working fairly fast. Speed should be read as a danger signal. So I put the parts of the table together—dry—and sat down to study them calmly, slowly. Then I moved my chair and looked from another point of view. The wide end's curved skirt was all right, but the long curve of the front edge looked somehow as though it needed a bit of help. (Or was it a touch of humor?) The upward curve of the grain pattern wasn't bad, although its effect could have been better. By a whim, or perhaps because I felt that it would give a little bit more legroom there, I added an upward curve of shape by making that skirt about three-eighths of an inch narrower toward its middle. No one else may notice this, but the thought of its being there is somehow enough for me, especially when the table looks right, as I believe it does.

While the table was assembled dry I made some patterns for the clamping blocks I needed in order to glue the parts together. At first I thought I could glue the two shorter ends and then the joints lengthwise, but then I realized that the blocks would slip that way. I would have to glue the two opposite joints at one time. So I made blocks notched for clamps that face one another; there is a double pressure on each block, which keeps it in place.

Even then, such gluing is a bit nerve-wracking, especially when one is alone. Before doing it, I worked the legs to their final shape—something that was a combination of intention, guesswork, and hope, a little bit here and a bit more there. I made the roundings successively smaller at the top and the bottom, with the maximum round at the point where the leg is thinnest. Such varied roundings are sensitive, and a great pleasure to do. I try to work them with

Gluing up: Special blocks, protective strip on inside, block with nailed-on cleats at each leg. All this and patience, too, just to do the actual gluing!

Mortises for spline tenons on curved parts of skirt. Piece at back of table has sawn tenons for ninety-degree joints.

cutting tools all the way, or nearly so, and if I sand them at all, or file them, it is very, very lightly. The more promising a piece seems, the more excited and afraid I am, so I dry-clamped the whole thing just once more. The back skirt, or stretcher, with its tenons, is in one piece; the stretcher at the short end, also in one piece, has double tenons to give added strength. Even without glue, the table did not shimmy.

Because of the drawer, the stretcher at the short end was a bit lower than the other three, and it flared a trifle less at that level. I made a mock-up of a drawer end itself, flared it to the shape of the top of the leg, put on the leaf, and looked again, wanting this end of the table to be as pleasing as the other.

Fear may not be a good thing, but caution certainly is. And I have developed the rule, or habit, of doing as much of the detail work on a piece as I can before gluing. Now I thought seriously about how the one drawer would work. I made the runners for this drawer and fitted them to the dry-clamped parts of the table. The solution, as you see, is very simple. I used a straightedge between the skirt tops to check that the height I was allowing with these runners was correct. And I used a piece of masonite, cut to the total width of the space between the legs at the short end, to get the runners parallel, with maybe just the slightest widening toward the far end where the back of the drawer was to be. I'm repeating myself, but it is worth remembering: A nice drawer glides easily, yet it grips a trifle just be-

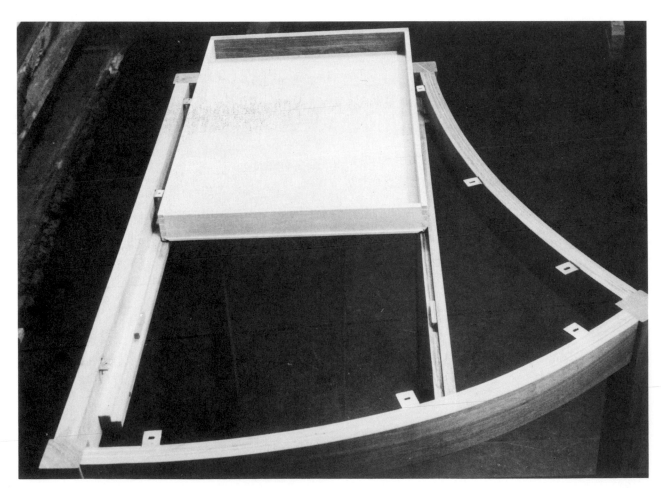

Drawer, slide rails, and stops were easier to fit with the table dry-clamped.

fore you pull it all the way out. There is real satisfaction in achieving this result, whether it's in an intricate cabinet or a relatively simple table. The time I took to check the measurements and fit the runners properly repaid itself in the final fitting of the drawer.

With the stand glued, I put on the top, and sat there, imagining that I was using the table. The curved edges, as they were, bit into my forearms; they needed to be softer and more friendly, but not simply rounded, as one is apt to assume. The two curved parts of the leaf are not so much rounded as they are softened—there is a sort of downhill feeling about them, perhaps not unlike the effect of long usage. Meanwhile, along its edges (thickness), the leaf has an outward flare corresponding to that of the legs. This flare is important; it is not lost because of the softness of the top edge. These are two distinct intentions, and I have tried to make them work together and yet preserve them as distinctly two. The one is the feeling of curve, an outward flare; the other (as you look at the top of the table) is the sense that these two curved edges, where one sits and works, are not hard, but have a friendliness about them that will be nice to experience by anyone sitting there.

Sturdy brass cleats for fastening tabletop: Those along the back edge have round holes; the rest are elongated.

Details of tabletop as they emerged.

Before fastening the top in place I needed to polish it, as well as the stand. How was I going to do this? Should I risk making the table considerably darker by the use of oil? Or should I leave it almost as light as the untreated wood, and use synthetic wax? I had, as usual, extra pieces of the various parts of that walnut plank. So I tried oil and an oil-based wax, a so-called antique wax. Also my synthetic "Renaissance" wax. The oil-based wax was what I wanted: not as dark as oil alone, but giving the wood a bit more color, or rather enhancing the color of the wood in a way that the Renaissance wax could not do. Looking back on this decision, I realize it was right; the marvelous walnut of the table is at its best treated with oil-based wax.

The drawer itself, the last piece of all, wasn't difficult to make. It is of fairly dark maple, and long—one can pull it out quite far without danger of its sagging. There is a recess with an undercut upper edge at the middle of the drawer front, quite handy as a grip, yet unobtrusive.

There are various ways of fastening a table leaf to the stand itself. If the skirt is fairly narrow, we can drill holes that are a bit oval and use screws. At other times little wood blocks with a lip that fit into corresponding grooves along the inside of the skirt are preferable. In this case I chose to make sturdy, L-shaped cleats of two-millimeter-thick brass. The ones at the straight back edge of the table have round holes, whereas the others have holes that are oval. This allows for a certain give-and-take of the leaf. And yet, with the screws pulled tight, the leaf is very firmly in place.

Reflecting on the way the table came about, I realize that I learned rather much going through the process. It was fun all the way after I had found that beautiful plank. I see, too, as it turned out, it is probably not the kind of table that should have been drawn. I won't say it could not have been drawn, although I know definitely that I could not have drawn it—or designed it, as they say.

Let us simply call it an illustration of composing, of having an idea and then letting it develop step by step. I did not quite trust myself until, at a certain point, I got the feeling that maybe, after all, this was a case where I was going to be lucky. And with that feeling, one usually *is* lucky.

Something I've thought about is how this table, or rather this particular situation, would turn out in another wood. It's not something I can predict, but I have the feeling that because I like it—the table *is* nice to use—I may return to it another time and try again with different wood. As a rough reminder, I have jotted down a few principal measurements on paper, cross sections, shapes, and a comment on how these might be changed or that they should not be changed. In another instance, when it is a cabinet or other straight-line piece and

measurements are what's mainly important, I make a measuring stick on which I mark the principal parts of the cabinet—not in numbers, but with little lines and arrows, and a few words, or sometimes just a figure to indicate the various parts. The old-timers used to do something similar.

They had in their shops these "measure-up" sticks with all sorts of lines and notations on them. Each of these quaint, dusty sticks of wood represented a piece of furniture. On these one had to make the proper notations from the beginning if one was to remember the meaning of it all.

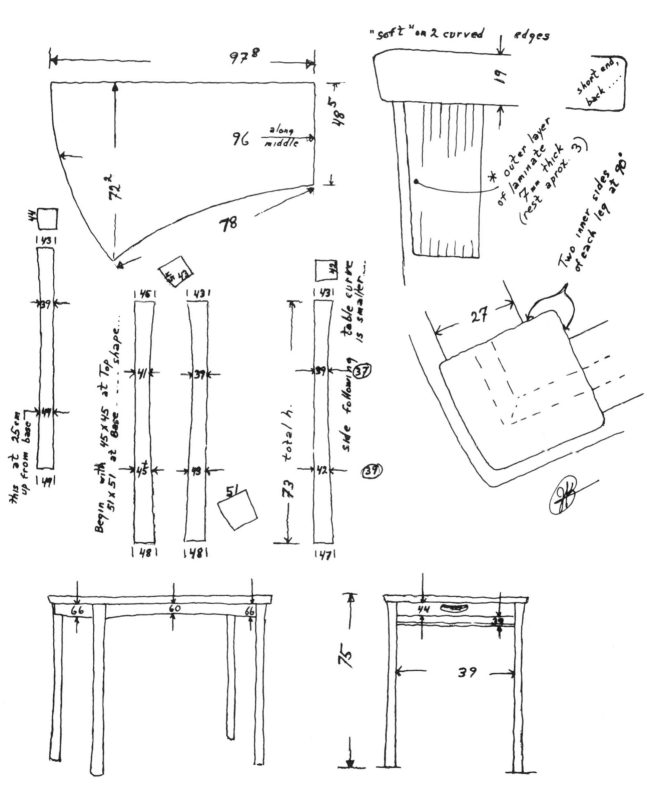

Left from my table I have now a piece of paper with measurements and curves, not too exact but fairly close to the actual piece. But I know already now that if I were to return to that table, it would be because the fact of another wood is an assurance that I won't make the table identical to the first one. I simply cannot duplicate anything. Each kind of wood, with its color and character and pattern, somehow—and fortunately—nudges me toward various deviations: small changes in the shape of a leg (because of the way the grain goes) or, maybe, increasing or decreasing the taper of that table leaf or changing the curve of it. These things will turn out differently with different woods. And I am very grateful for this because it is what will encourage me to try again.

Writing table of Italian walnut. Finished with oil-based wax. 1978.

Carved Curves

Here is a cabinet in Oregon pine. This is the second of these cabinets. The first, or "original" one was in elm and came on an impulse, more as a way of working than as a design or even as an idea. I had been doing something very exacting, a showcase with minute details, and by the time I finished it I was very tired. I really needed a rest. But instead of a rest in the ordinary sense, I suppose what I wanted was a different way to work. I needed to carve, to shape pieces, instead of mostly fitting them. From that need, and what was really an impulse, came the cabinet in elm.

This was about a year earlier. Now, in connection with an exhibition in Copenhagen, I wanted to try once more. I had some wonderful English brown oak—large planks of it. Oak is similar in its mood to elm, and the first cabinet had been good. So I decided on oak and began to saw up the pieces. I knew the color of the cabinet would be different; also the pattern and grain of the oak were different from that of the elm. So there would be something to look forward to. But in its basic mood I hoped that the oak would suit this piece.

I got into the work, started to saw the wood for the sides. And, to make a long story short, I missed doing my cabinet in oak by about half an inch! Really. Because at a point where I would saw the curve of one of the sidepieces there emerged a honeycomb, one of those horrid results of still

more horrid drying of wood. I say "emerged," since it really was impossible to discover it before I had sawn into the shape. Usually I saw outside the line I have made, allowing a bit of a margin; I did so this time, and ran into that honeycomb. I tried another cut, closer to the line, with very little margin; still the ugly crack was there. I made a third cut, and planed my way right down to a minimum measurement—this *had* to be all right. But no, the fault persisted. I had another plank or two of oak, and I did open one more—and again there were checks and honeycombs, driving me to the point of desperation. I was sad, and terribly angry, cursed those people in England at the large, "reputable" firm that had dried the wood so brutally.

For some days I was knocked out. Still, I wanted that cabinet. The way of work it represented was right for me then, and people did like the first piece. So I tried again, this time in Oregon pine. I had a number of pieces of this wood which I'd chosen very carefully some years earlier. It was close-grained and straight. The quality of close grain was important to me because I knew that to get the nice shapes I wanted out of a wood like Oregon pine with its "hard-soft" variances—the tendency to "waves" when cut—I had to begin with a piece that was close-grained, nice and smooth.

I was tired when I began, and, although the Oregon pine appealed to me, there was somewhere a slight doubt as to whether it would go well with the shapes and the proportions I was about to try. Was it lively enough? I'd made a cabinet of this wood for a violinist some years before that was straight-lined and strict. There the wood certainly did suit the piece. But here? The facts that I was tired and the wood easy to work were a poor excuse. Yet, at that moment, had I chosen a more difficult wood, a harder or more unpredictable wood where I'd have to saw and resaw around cracks and knots, I don't think I would have had the strength to do it.

I started to saw the Oregon pine, and my mood improved; it was sweet wood. I wasn't so uncertain any more, although I suppose I should have been, because from the time I started shaping the sides everything somehow became different. I found myself allowing more in certain places, making the sides just a trifle longer and a bit deeper. Perhaps it was the softness of the wood, or the color of it, or both. I'm not sure, but something was happening: I was making these allowances. Already I had a hint that this second cabinet would not be quite the same as the first.

Idea-sketches for cabinet in elm, later also made in Oregon pine.

I had a slip of paper with the principal measurements of the piece as it had been in elm, and I referred to these, though not without some doubt. I roughly shaped the sides and set them up and made a mock-up using pieces that represented the top and bottom and some very thin plywood for the doors. "Redoing" this piece as I now was, I knew something of the relationships of the doors to the cabinet sides, one shape dependent upon the other. Earlier, with the piece in elm, I had had no clear sense of how the doors would fit along the front edge of the cabinet sides. These shapes, which resulted in the compound curve of the doors, came to me only after I had set up the sides on the cabinet and made a first mock-up of the doors. My original idea called for simple convex doors, but the way I had to bend the plywood to meet the cabinet sides showed me the doors should have another and different curve, too. This was a practical lesson and confirmed again the fact that for me this is the right way to work. I have a great deal to learn. Although I try to use my past experiences, I am a very eager and, in a way, impatient person; I'm apt to overlook certain dangers and facts. But this step-by-step method, with its unpredictables and its revelations, shows me where to go, where I am headed, and I am sure it has helped me to avoid many a catastrophe.

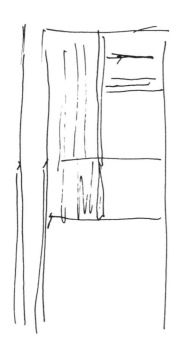 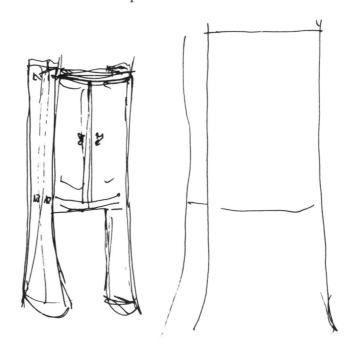

The two cabinets: in elm (left) and in pine (right).

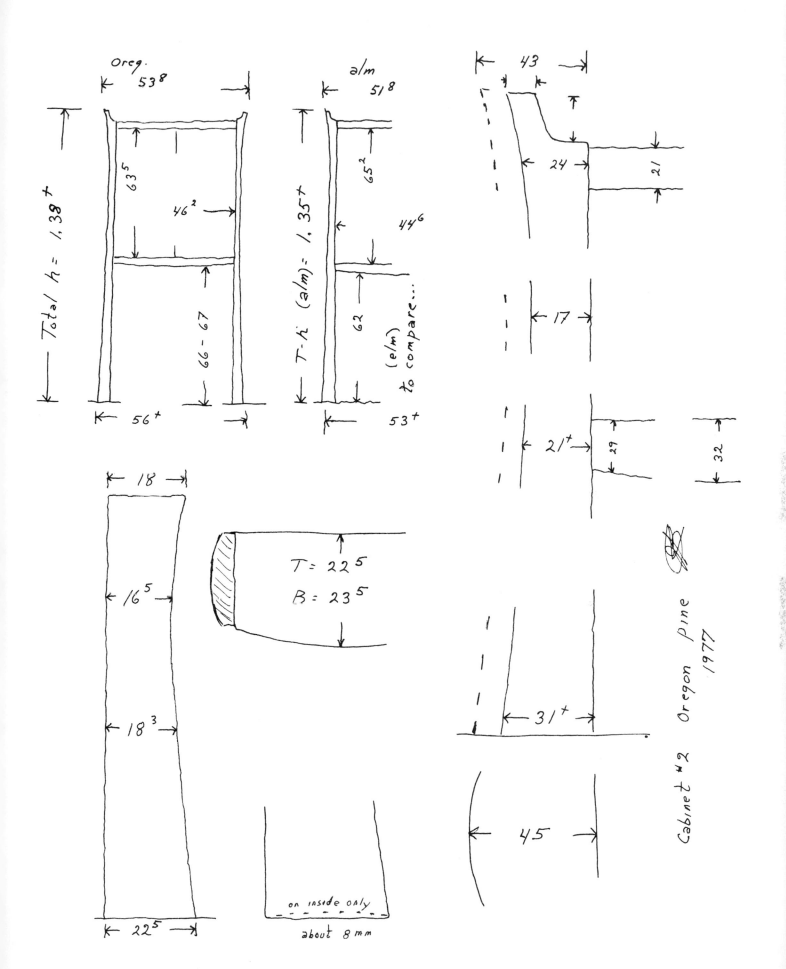

Oreg.
538

a/m
518

Total h = 1,38+

63⁵

46²

66 - 67

56+

T-h (a/m) = 1,35+

65²

44⁶

(e/m)
to compare...

62

53+

43

24

21

17

21+

29

32

31+

45

Cabinet #2   Oregon Pine
1977

18

16⁵

18³

22⁵

T = 22⁵
B = 23⁵

on inside only

about 8mm

89

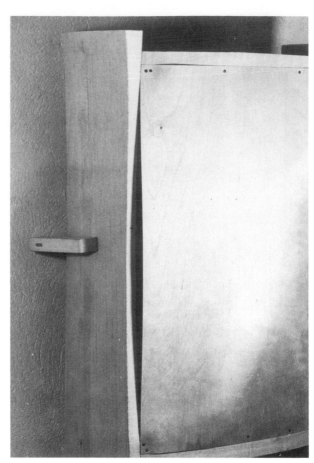

Various setups for cabinet in Oregon pine.

Discovering details: Thin plywood representing doors shows how convex curve becomes compound where it meets the cabinet sides.

As I say, I began with measurements and experiences from the first cabinet. I next placed the horizontals representing the top and bottom in a similar way and chose a width very close to that of the "original." I looked, and it simply did not make sense. There was a clumsiness about the body part—that is, the doors. Its volume in relation to the sidepieces was wrong. The first setup I chose was unbalanced *in that particular wood*. I saw I had to change it, jotted down some notes about this choice, reshuffled things a bit—making the door part shorter—and looked again. Result: I had to narrow the cabinet somewhat to compensate for having shortened the doors! Gradually—in the course of about four setups—I was able to arrive at something I felt began to make sense. The influence of the first cabinet began to let go; it became a comparison rather than a compulsion. I really was beginning all over again! Instead of being a disappointment, this made me happy, gave me new energy. Someone said somewhere: It isn't the arriving, it's the journey. I had begun a new journey with this piece. Oh, I did hope to arrive. Now I feel that the enjoyment of the journey adds to the joy of arriving.

It was fun to compare the new measurements, as they emerged, with those of the first piece. I had jotted down the others in ink, and now I used a colored pen to put down the measurements of the new piece—a centimeter or two shorter here, a bit wider there. Looking back, it was, I realize, a lesson in how color and grain affect the proportions, and also the volume, of a piece. This cabinet was of a new size and weight, but *not* because of any numbers. The new dimensions only confirmed the fact that the cabinet was taking form in a different way, while all I was doing was looking for something I could believe in, that was promising, and would be even better as I went

along. There are those who insist it is possible to measure one's way to beautiful (successful?) things. Thank God this is not so—at least not in wood. Aesthetics deals not with certainties, but with search.

Only the unexpectedly light color of the wood bothered me a little. I knew a bit about Oregon pine, and I like the reddish color that comes to this wood with time. I hoped this color would help my cabinet a bit, later on. As things turned out, it did.

Encouraged by what the mock-up promised, I got into the work itself. You can see how the wood for the top and bottom pieces was selected: the top has the grain sloping down and in, the bottom up and in. As I sawed this to my curves, I got the soft downward and upward sweeps that help one to experience the cabinet as a calm whole. Even if the grain is subdued—as it is in this wood—the lines with their intention are there. At this point, however, I left the top and bottom pieces whole—that is, straight along their front edge—since I could not quite predict the final shape or curves of the doors here. These doors are what one might call *carved shapes*. From

Choice of grain along front of top and bottom pieces: This often involves beginning with extra width to "straighten out" the direction of the grain and achieve a balanced final pattern. Although it is still evident in close-grained wood, the cabinet in elm shows this more clearly.

a single curve at the middle, each door gradually flows into a compound curve at the outside, where it meets the cabinet side. I made a template of the shape along the front edge; this helped me to judge how thick the outer parts—about one-third of each door width—should be. I bandsawed these to a very rough shape, twisting as I cut, to save some unnecessary carving. Before gluing I made sure—once, twice—that the doors together would be wide enough when in their proper positions. The compound curves, at the point where they meet the cabinet sides, must be trimmed at a specific angle—they must be exactly parallel. A bit tricky, since they fit in only one position; pivot them slightly, and a widening slit appears where there should be a good fit.

The outside part of each door is formed to a compound curve. This requires extra thickness, roughly bandsawn to shape before it is glued onto the rest of the coopered shape.

Another margin I had to consider early was the overlap of the doors at the middle. To avoid having to later glue a piece onto the left-hand door for the rabbet I had to have about five-sixteenths of an inch extra width here.

Having glued up the doors, I planed and spokeshaved them to a preliminary shape, allowing for the thickness toward the outside edge where each would fit the sidepiece. Here something occurred that's worth remembering. I was working away, clean-cutting the inside of slick Oregon pine with one of my rounded planes (which, by the way, are not roughing planes, but planes that, with the right wood, give a shimmering finish to the shape). From the center edge of the door and out about two-thirds of the way across, the curve is simple, and here I was using just straight-on strokes, the usual rock-as-you-cut motion,

*Doors are finished with planes and spokeshave only
and are left unsanded.*

obvious enough. But then, as I got into the outer part, where the compound or double curve begins, the cuts became uneven. And felt wrong. "Maybe the iron is dull," I told myself. No, it was not. Then something happened: The shape of the door began talking to the plane in my hands. I found myself cutting, not straight along as before, but in a sweep, pivoting from the waist with an easy motion. The tool followed the surface and was cutting clean all the way. Now, why I had not I thought . . . Thought, I say here, realizing only now a simple truth: I did not *think*; I didn't change my motion as a result of *thought*. That is the secret and the satisfaction.

Before cutting the doors to length, I made the lip and rabbet at the middle. After this, a cross-cut at what was to be the bottom of each door. Because of their shape, it was easier to do this on the bandsaw and then carefully plane each end square and true. I set up the two doors on the flat jointer table in their "proper" curve.

When doing something like this, you can do it either by eye or with a cardboard template of the final line you want. Check the total width—but generously, using a measuring stick that fits inside the cabinet. Avoid numbers!

With the toward-the-middle part of each door as a guide, I table-sawed these to an even width, remembering that the left-hand door, with its rabbet, needs to be about five-sixteenths of an inch *wider* than the right-hand one. I used a supporting wood strip under the door where it followed the long table saw fence to lift it to the position it would have when in the cabinet; in other words—and this is important—the strip represents the total inside depth of the door curves. I set the saw very cautiously, allowing about one-sixteenth inch in width on each door half. I worked slowly, pressing evenly against the fence, and then bandsawed the doors to lengths "just too tight," and finally very neatly planed them (square!) to an even, snug fit in the cabinet. Widthwise they had only started to fit, be-

ing still a bit too wide. Kept in position along the overlap middle, they did tend to bulge outward a little. Notice how they relate to the cabinet sides. Cautiously I trimmed them in—step by step, a little at a time. This is a "different" sort of cabinet—odd doors and a somewhat special fit—so I took my time, working the edges, outside, top, and bottom a trifle at a try. When the fit was right at each outside, there was also that hair-fine tolerance along the top and bottom edges. And the curve is as we want it: as the doors are fitted they move into line at the middle and that angular part is gone.

So far so good. I traced the desired outer curves of the door on the cabinet top and bottom; took the piece apart, sawed the top and bottom to their shapes, allowing about one-eighth inch for rounded edges.

Now I could locate my hinges and fit their halves into the cabinet. Despite the fact that this was my second such piece, I nearly made a fatal mistake. I was about to fit the **L**-shaped hinge halves all around when, at the last moment, I remembered—oops!—the ones at the bottom had to be not **L**-shaped, but *straight, facing inward*, and parallel to the cabinet side. Why? Look closely at the photos! While one half of each hinge is snug against the cabinet side and—so to say—in line with its inside, its counterpart on the door, which curves out and away from that line, results in a fit that does not allow one to slide this door part of the hinge into place when hanging the doors. So one has to have some other sliding or slip-in access, in this case our straight hinge half in the cabinet bottom. In words this sounds confusing; illustrations are better here. Let them also be a reminder of a particular solution, adding to the variety of uses for knife-type hinges. The main thing is to think before going too far in one's eagerness, as I nearly did.

Because of the peculiar shape of the doors and the way they fit the flat insides of the cabinet, fitting the hinges involved some hazardous cuts.

Having come so far without accident, my confidence in the cabinet was growing. I felt good even about the more trying part of the work. I had earlier bandsawed roughly the form of the top edges of each side; now I carved each to its final shape, not identical, but similar to each other. The carving was pleasant, although by no means easy; even with a sharp chisel, Oregon pine is difficult to cut across the grain. One of my curved knives helped me get the finishing with-the-grain cuts I needed.

Prior to gluing the case together, I went over all its surfaces with my finest planes and a Kunz spokeshave set to a very fine cut. And though Oregon pine may seem an easy wood on which to get a smooth surface, it really is not; there is a tendency to raise, to "irritate," the grain to a fuzz. So planing and spokeshaving, too, demand patience.

After I had glued up the case, actually without having left any bad marks on its surfaces, and done the backpiece with its panel of wavy-patterned Lebanon cedar, I refitted the doors to mark them for their hinge halves. There was a little wind to correct as a result of vague human factors—present always—as I had done the shapes. The margin of thickness I had allowed along the outside of each door was good to have now; I could lightly plane the doors to their final curves and fit. In doing so, I found that their shape changed a trifle; here and there it departed from the shaped edges of the cabinet top and bottom. So I had to very gingerly—reminding myself to take plenty of time—redo these top and bottom curves with a spokeshave, block plane, and file. I covered the adjacent side edges of the cabinet with taped-on bits of cardboard. By then I really had some interests to protect:

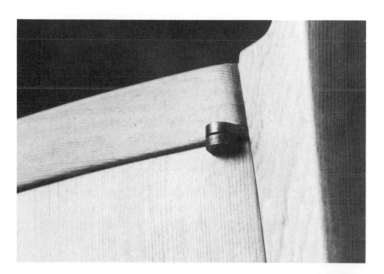

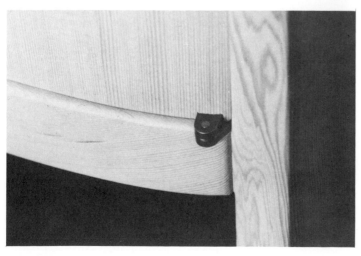

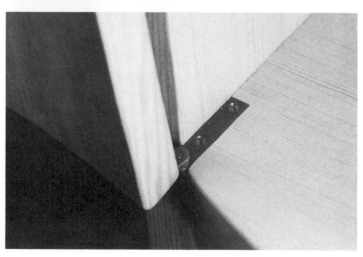

I could use force on myself, if necessary, to keep me cautious. In a situation like this you simply have to be on good terms with time. . . .

Fitting those **L**-shaped hinge halves to the doors was a bit tense. One wants to be rested, alone, and pulled together. I know this was an odd way to do it. I could have had special hinges made, with the corner of each **L** at a specific angle; this would allow a slip-on fit—I realize that. But I did not have such hinges on hand and getting them made is a time-consuming bother. Besides, the shape of the doors and each corner angle is not finally and exactly predictable. The unpredictability of such details is to me a sensible one; it belongs to making

the piece, to the curves as they grow. And because I like all this process of taking shape, I have to work accordingly and arrive sometimes at solutions that may, later on, seem unnecessarily difficult, but which, at the time, fitted the work and the way the piece was forming itself.

With a very sharp scribe I marked the thickness of the hinge where it protrudes from the door. There were a few tiny, sensitive first cuts to make with a chisel, the rest was patience. Which meant remembering to use specially shaped blocks or pieces of cork each and every time I handled the cabinet sides or clamped the doors in the bench vise, which was rather often. And later, when gluing, I had to fit the blocks carefully to

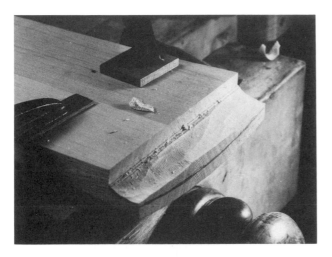

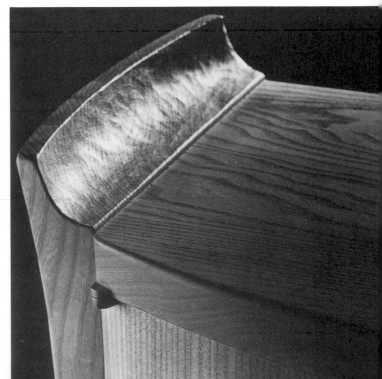

Sidepieces: Shaping the top with a chisel and then finishing along the grain with a curved knife (made from a pattern-maker's file).

the areas where the joints were and then line them with cardboard. Oregon pine is soft wood, easily damaged beyond repair.

One of the facts of working this way is that besides wanting a piece pleasing in its proportions and with certain other appealing details of workmanship, one wants it also to be unblemished, to have a definite clarity and neatness. So the least damage to the piece, even though others may overlook it, is a personal setback to the craftsman. Ah, vanity! With a cabinet like this, delicacy is not so much a matter of size as it is of the nature of the wood itself. Although we may not always regard it as such, Oregon pine is a delicate wood. One wrong cut, and there goes perfection. I had a bad half day fitting those hinge parts. I suppose it's like a surgeon having to operate on a good friend, or his own child. . . .

With the cabinet glued and those doors fitted, I could come down to the shop, look at the piece, and get the feeling it was going to be all right, if . . . If I could get the handles the right size, and in the right place. If the cabinet would mellow, changing shade as I hoped it would. I was nearly home, and yet still there were those ifs.

The handles, this time, are a bit lower on the doors than on the first cabinet. Also they are slightly larger. Again this is the result not so much of planning as of a feel—the cabinet, with its light wood, asked for larger handles. The wood in these is something that a friend of mine, Joseph Tracy, found in a Florida swamp. Driving along, he saw these gnarled dead trees—some sort of ironwood, I suppose, a distant relative of lignum vitae, I'd guess by the wood. So now I have this cabinet, and it is of Oregon pine with its backpiece of cedar from Lebanon and its door handles of a strange unnamed wood from a Florida swamp.

I don't know whether I will ever do this cabinet again. I just might, because the nature of the work itself, with this composing, adjusting to a particular wood, doing so much cutting and carving by hand, is very beneficial to a high-strung person like myself who often does meticulous, straight-line work. So I may return to this cabinet in another wood, another mood—with the result being different measurements and another little adventure. There are a few pieces that I like to redo for very special reasons: for the way of work and, I hope, the result.

The silver chest—an exception—I do for the result, almost in spite of the methods involved, because there the work itself is a tremendous strain, requiring phenomenal self-discipline, step by intricate step. I have returned to this silver chest only because on a few occasions I have found new and different wood that made me believe each time that perhaps now, now, I would make *the* silver chest. And I think I have done so. In 1977, I made the one in American maple: the case spalted, the drawers of bird's-eye. This chest has something very special about it. It is more ethereal and refined than its predecessors. The stand is a bit higher, the drawer handles have a subtle, at first unintended little rib or shading down their middle. There are other details, too, that came off especially well: the through joints, for example, are not finished flush as they were in the earlier stands.

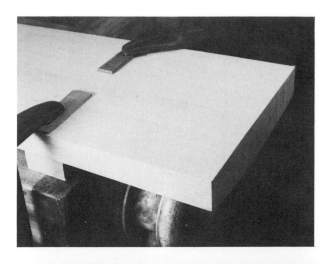

So this is a rather special silver case. And it is the last. I know I cannot make it better, so this has to be the last one . . . *finito*.

Two months have passed since I made the cabinet in Oregon pine. Along with several other pieces it is in my workshop, waiting for the journey to Copenhagen. And, yes, it is all right. Right now I think it is as good as the one in elm, although that may be because the actual feeling of the work on this cabinet is still with me, satisfying in its own particular way.

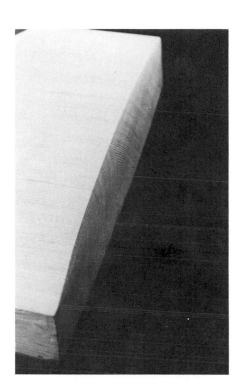

The inside of the cabinet sidepiece at the base proved stiff to the eye. Shaping it—on the inside only—helped restore the soft rhythm of the whole piece.

A Playful Thing

This may be one of the few pieces of which someone will one day say, "That's not like his work at all." An intriguing thought. Here is the way the thing came about:

I was going through some old clippings when I saw an article with a photograph of a piece that I had made about fifteen years earlier. It was an odd "showcase" cabinet, odd because there was no glass. Seeing the old photo, I was reminded of the piece. And again, as I had fifteen years ago, I liked the mood of it. That first cabinet, as I saw it now, had a weak point; the enclosed (wood) part—that is to say, the body—extending almost to the floor, was a bit heavy. Otherwise, it was a pleasant piece with its combination of lemonwood and doussie, beige and brown colors that mellowed so nicely with the years.

The playfulness of that no-glass showcase came back to me now with its original force. At the same time I wanted to start anew. I put away the photo, closed my eyes, keeping only the thought. . . . Except for an idea I believed in, I started from scratch. And from the start, maybe I had a dual feeling: I wanted a lighter and more airy effect, a small body rather high up off the floor and then this space, which I imagine as a sort of theater or stage for little things. There was going to be a feeling of lightness, but it would be definite, clean-lined, not soft. I imagined the wood in the frame as being very hard,

and dark. The rest—surfaces—would be milder, but in tune with the dark frame. I had a large piece of East Indian rosewood that I'd bought several years before; it was dry, and it was unusual in that it had very straight grain. It really was an excellent piece, about five and a half feet long. There were no checks at the ends and, since the wood was dry, I realized that there would be no further trouble—I could use practically the entire length, which I did need. Yes, I liked that rosewood! Already I was thinking about the other wood to go with it. I brought out some fine steamed pearwood, a piece of mahogany, also some real Andaman padouk. All these woods seemed to go well with the rosewood. But as yet I did not have to decide which I would use.

So I concentrated on the rosewood and the framework of a cabinet about which I had only a very vague notion and a few sketches —mere questions around the idea. The construction of the piece—the four legs (we'll call them posts) and the frames—is a bit unusual. It depends upon the posts' being set at forty-five degrees. From past experience I knew that when one plans such a construction in all its various parts, one is dependent upon two factors: the size of the surfaces on the forty-five degree bevels that are the two insides of the posts; and, directly related, the principal dimensions of the legs, their maximum width and depth. There is a very definite relationship there. When you decide on one, the other adjusts itself

Sawing East Indian rosewood for posts of cabinet.
Support, clamped onto sawhorse, has roller made
from plexiglass rod; when not in use, it is easily
stored away.

to that. If you study the sketches and the photographs, you will see how this is true. Another consideration here: Because the stretchers are at forty-five-degree angles, the point of pressure is along a specific line through the post. We cannot extend the post out—that is to say, in its depth—too far, since we are then beyond the proper line of pressure, and there will be a twisting as we clamp the joints tight. There is a very real risk of breakage.

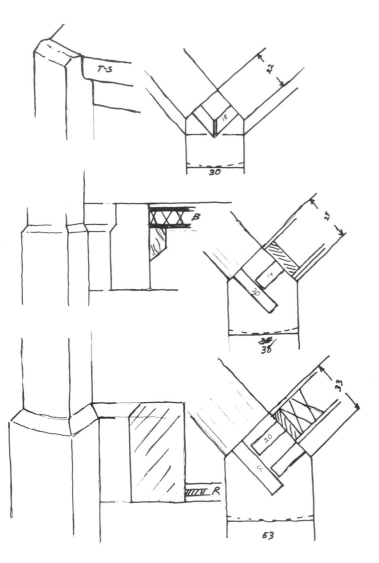

Construction: The basic idea involving parts set at a forty-five-degree angle.

Clamping: Special blocks (with pieces of forty-five-degree-angle strips left after posts are sawn) are held on clamps with rubber bands. Care must be taken in planning such constructions to clamp tightly without risking twist, and breakage.

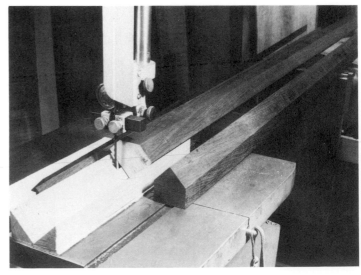

Setting up for forty-five-degree cuts on insides of posts.

102

The guess I made as to the size of the posts was probably some kind of lines-and-volumes notion I had regarding this cabinet with its three main parts: the lower space beginning from the floor; then the rather light, smallish body; and finally the "stage," or play place, that is the top third. Down low, the piece needed sturdy legs, fairly thick in their dimensions. Then there would be a graduated decrease in size in the two other parts. One, two, three: thick, thinner, and quite thin. So I sawed four posts from that big heavy piece of rosewood. Besides this I had some scrap pieces from other work. With these I clamped up a first guess of what the cabinet might be. It didn't tell me very much, except that I had to guess again, to move the legs closer together, farther apart . . . then those thin pieces, which represented various stretchers, a little bit up; no, a little bit down. . . . With the posts unshaped, everything was rather vague. At one setup the stretchers around what would be the body part seemed well placed; if I moved them up or down, my doubts increased. I felt that with the body *there*, the rest might arrange itself. So I made some marks—two on each post—for the step, or the changeover from one thickness to the next, although I didn't cut these as yet.

I bandsawed the two forty-five-degree bevels on each post. Immediately they seemed a good deal less awkward. I clamped my setup again, about as I had marked it, and played with it some more. Yes, there was a promise. I was fairly eager, but worried, too, because I realized that the cabinet, with the constructions it called for, was going to be a lot of work. Definitely, this was a difficult piece. I was on the way to something as uncertain as it was unusual for me.

Guessing the way with the help of posts before and after they have been shaped.

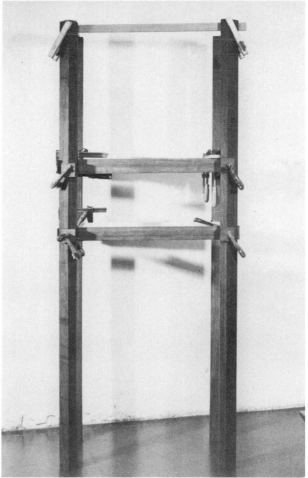

Looking at those clamped-up pieces and trying to decide whether or not to go on, I suppose I felt like a person who is about to build a house, but who has no drawings: the outcome of the house probably depends upon how the framework takes shape. I bandsawed the two outer cuts, which, with their bevels, would result in the different dimensions of the posts. I made the short (middle section) cut first. Then, without removing the wood there, I sawed the long cut, so that I still had the wood against the guide, after which I simply cut away those two sections at a bevel and cleaned them up with a sharp chisel.

At about this time my head was sort of turned forty-five degrees, thinking and seeing at that angle. I had to make special troughs or blocks to support the lengths as I worked on them, and did various plans (or layouts), also on an across-the-corner basis. Everything for a few days was forty-five degrees. Angles that didn't suit old habits, corners that seemed odd. . . .

Maybe that was one reason why I began to react against the sharp outer edges of the posts; I felt a future unfriendliness there. At any rate, I found myself softening these. As you see in the photographs, there is a slight radius—a rounding—no more than two or three millimeters, actually. But notice the difference it makes! I experienced it doing the cutting, a kind of transformation of shape and of feeling, just because of a few millimeters. Similar details have crept into my work through the years. Mere trifles—yet how well remembered!

Rather often I refer to little discoveries that come—not from drastic shapes and the need for eccentricity—but through small questioning touches. Observing various influences and trends—the current flashy idioms as compared to softer expressions—I do feel that sooner or later there will be a lesser need for exaggerations and a greater realization of the satisfactions inherent in various subtleties. I think that because certain people have not helped us, we have simply neglected to look properly at our work. By this I mean not analytically or according to some guide, but simply with sensitive eyes.

By now I was optimistic about the posts. This put me in a good mood. Although I was still teetering between two feelings: promise and doubt. The placement of the enclosed part of the cabinet looked all right; the other two parts seemed fairly well related to it, which made me optimistic. At the same time, I was getting into the details of construction. I sensed the difficulties there, and some-

Outside of post at midsection: Shape as first sawn (flat) and then with a slight radius—about 3/16"—done by hand. So little and yet so much. . . .

times I would stop, full of doubt, and just say to myself: "It's an unusual and maybe promising thing. It might turn out fairly well. But will it turn out well enough?"

As the amount of effort here grew more apparent, the chances of fulfilling my hopes became less certain. One can want to do a thing, and believe in it—that still doesn't tell one whether it is worth doing. We can weigh the work realistically—in terms of time, material, and so forth—and yet be left with doubt, or fear, that the piece will not live up to the whole of what we want, won't justify itself. And by this I do not mean in terms of time or money.

Such doubts are increased by the sheer effort of certain work, the awkward size and weight of pieces of wood, the need for supports when working them, the complexity of a construction with its demands for concentration . . . and work, work—always only you alone with it.

I got some help from the rosewood; its smooth grain and wonderful texture were a pleasure to handle. By now I had looked several times at my other woods and decided that the Andaman padouk would go beautifully with my rosewood. This again put me in a state of hopeful excitement. I had a drawing, very simple, of the areas of the leg that involved various joints. The dimensions of these were only approximate,

but I could see the way the stretchers met, and could plan the joints there. Because of how the stretchers are aligned at each of two levels, and the nature of the legs with their bevels, I could not have two long tenons meeting at any given corner. One had to be long, the other shorter. I decided that the stretchers on the long sides of the cabinet, which are strengthened by panels, could be shorter. But I would double them—two fairly short tenons. The stretchers at the short end of the piece, where there is no other support, would be single and as long as possible, which in this case is fairly long. At this stage of actual "building," I was thinking of strength and trying to balance my constructions accordingly. You know, it is easy for any of us to be so excited about the looks of a piece and a new idea that we forget, or pay less attention to, the importance of the piece being strong and able to stand up to all kinds of wear. Trying to overcome this, I am perhaps overly aware of the need for strength. Although, here, too much is the better of two extremes.

The joints needed not only strength but exactness, because the position of the stretchers with the panel had to be precise, as did that of the shorter stretchers. Between them would be the drawers, so any upward or downward shifting of the stretchers would result in the spaces being uneven and make the fitting of the drawers difficult or impossible to do well. So I worked on my horizontal mortiser for a while, using those clean-cutting end mills I've talked about. Then I cut the tenons very carefully on the table saw. Because I wanted strong joints and was aware my hard, fine rosewood had no give-and-take, I found the patience and had the luck to make them exact. This simplified the work later on. And I want to point out here: This work, done on my simple machines, did not take "too much" time. Also, no matter what talk about skill, one cannot and should not make such joints by hand only, except in a very, very exceptional case—perhaps with softer wood.

With the framework dry-clamped I took a piece of the padouk and tried it for color in the space that was to be panelled. And yes, it was wonderful. So I sawed four pieces of veneer, each piece in one whole width, for the two sides of the cabinet and glued these on bonded solid-wood core. There was a bit of nervous work where a panel had to fit exactly the space between the stretchers, as well as lengthwise between the posts. I got it fairly right; to make sure that it would stay right when gluing I made two splines on the long edges in both stretcher and panel. Then, as is apt to happen when working with hardwood, something made me feel the need for a softness, or friendliness, of touch. I rather often feel a need to achieve a play between hard and soft. Now I not so much rounded as softened the edges of the panel where it meets the posts and

Mortise-and-tenon joints, double and single, must fit snugly without risk of shifting. This gives exact space for drawers and rails.

stretchers. This isn't a real rounding or a bevel, but only the beginning of what might have been a rounded shape. I can describe it only as soft, or friendly. It isn't all that noticeable at a distance. It's more a feeling than a definite shape. A shading—that's it; there is a barely discernable shift there, as one comes closer there is a play of light along the edges where the reddish padouk meets the dark rosewood. And this shading is pleasant; since the cabinet is quite angular and straight-lined, it needs a softer touch here and there.

These details "just happen" when one is guided by feelings, guesses, or whatever else you want to call them. Later on, they are confirmed by common sense, someone simply saying, "That's nice."

Care has its rewards. With the panel parts in place and the joints of the two short end stretchers accurately done, I could locate and then rout grooves for the drawer runners. I tried to be very accurate; in a way, I suppose, I was accurate. Still, there was a human element in my accuracy—small deviations, a fraction of a millimeter up or down. So that later on I had to do a bit of extra fitting with those drawers to get them right.

Thus far I had not done any detailed thinking about the part we can call the roof—the top of the cabinet—except to try to determine in my setups its rough proportions. Now I dry-clamped some strips up there once more, trying various dimensions, and atop these I placed still other narrow pieces representing the thickness of the roof itself. Small changes in dimensions made a lot of difference here. So did any increase or decrease in the overhang of the roof as it related to the supports or stretchers under it. This was a question of a bit more, a tiny bit less, just as it had been with the framework.

And as with the other parts of the cabinet, its final location wasn't the result of certainty. It turned out to be near my various guesses—yes, I had made pencil marks, but on dark wood these show badly and are quickly smudged away. I'd thought, "This

is a bit low and that is too high," had moved things, made those marks. And yet, well along on the cabinet, with things "in place," satisfied, I realized that the final position of the stretchers, for instance, was neither exactly *on* any of my markings, nor definitely *between* them. It wasn't as if I'd said, "This is an inch too high, that is an inch too low, we'll put it halfway between," although maybe that was partly true. Yet something else was at work; let's leave it at that. The placement of the pieces is not all to my credit. I don't mind admitting that.

Top of post with mortises. The step to take the "roof" has a carefully rounded corner.

107

There are joints, again at forty-five degrees, not very large, for the stretchers supporting the roof. If these look weak, remember that when the roof is placed atop the stretchers, and glued there, the whole structure locks itself; it definitely is strong. Besides, we're not going to land helicopters up there. The

veneered roof itself, and also the part I will call the floor (the base surface of the show space) are two sawn widths of veneer on each side, glued onto Baltic plywood. There are fairly wide edge gluings on the roof part, because at the corners where it meets the posts, there is a forty-five-degree bevel (notice that this is rounded on the underside). I wanted the edge gluings to meet just inside that bevel. I needed their width, because the overlap of the roof is hardly one-half inch here, and thin edge gluings would expose the padouk on the underside. These details, as I now explain them, seem perhaps rather contrived, as if there had been a tremendous amount of figuring before each step. One does think, but without great strain; things arrange themselves. Maybe this is experience. Maybe it is luck. Probably it is a combination of both. As a rule, when I am into a thing that I believe in and that excites me, I work fairly well. My logic then is as a certain level of efficiency. Deep in the work, I worry less.

Top part of the cabinet changes character as details form themselves.

When it came to the drawer handles, I was unsure; I guessed at a few shapes and glued these onto pieces of padouk veneer, which represented the drawer fronts. What I was looking for was a shape not only pleasing to the eye, but fitted to the purpose as well. One may say this is quite obvious, and yet not everyone approaches the matter with such double intent. There are shapes fine to look at, but not quite as good to use; they do not feel right between the fingers or in the hand. The drawers are fairly large and run both ways through the cabinet case. The way one pulls or pushes them usually calls for slipping the forefinger under the handle and holding the thumb atop it. The resulting shape feels right when one uses the drawers, either to push or to pull. These handle shapes are not machined. Only the tenon has been done on the circular saw, the rest is carved. It's nice work with small tools and fine wood. That feeling of fine wood is, I hope, present in the entire cabinet. The drawer sides and bottom are of extremely close-grained mahogany, probably real Cuban. (Some of my woods I have obtained in small pieces, and I am not always certain as to their origin, since they reach me by odd ways, often having lain for years in obscure places.)

The padouk and the rosewood have this sense of hardness and smoothness about them, too. One would not want to put oil finish on such colors and textures, so the panels are only slightly waxed with my English synthetic wax, as are the legs and framework. None of the surfaces is glossy, there is only a satiny sense of clear, hard wood and delicate colors. If you touch the wood, you can sense the hardness—the friendliness, too. And if you knock on it, you get that firm, quality sound. Cabinetmaker's music.

I become emotional about these things, not only when I'm working, but already when the idea comes to me. And later; when I've made the piece, I'm apt to have a letdown: I am unsure whether my emotions exceeded my common sense. Although I've never been able to finish anything that I didn't believe in, after making this cabinet I was a little bit afraid. Not disappointed; no, I liked it. It stood there in the downstairs workshop for some days, and I would come down and look at it and walk around it. One or two close friends visited me, and they enjoyed it. Still, the very unusualness of it made me a little bit apprehensive. What would people think? Maybe a craftsman isn't supposed to care; maybe what we do is important only in relation to ourselves. I don't know. But I do care about what people think. Or rather, I care about what a certain kind of person will think and feel. People with whom I have an affinity, or for whom I have a great respect, I set in a certain relationship to what I make. So it does matter to me. I cannot say, "Well, I made it and I like it, so be hanged!" Or, "I made it, it's interesting, someone will buy it, and that's what matters."

We took the piece from the shop and up to the living room. There, with pinkish light coming through the curtains and more space around it, the cabinet really seemed to enjoy itself. For a while we played with that space, or stage, or whatever one may call the upper part. We could have the cabinet rather far from the wall, and walk around it, and look at the objects "in" it, and maybe take them out and then replace them in another way. And when viewed from a sitting position in the room, the cabinet still looked nice. This was especially pleasing to me, because such a piece is apt to be better when viewed from one height than from another.

The cabinet is still with us. People have come and gone and thought different things about it. I myself like it—in a secret sort of way. It was done, not in a spirit of contradiction—well, not exactly—but somehow, perhaps indirectly, to disprove all this about Krenov making curved doors and showcases with glass and pieces that have all their surfaces hand-planed. It's a different kind of a piece, even for me. And I enjoy the sense of that difference. It gives me a relaxed, playful feeling, and with my tendency to be too serious this is something that I need, now and then.

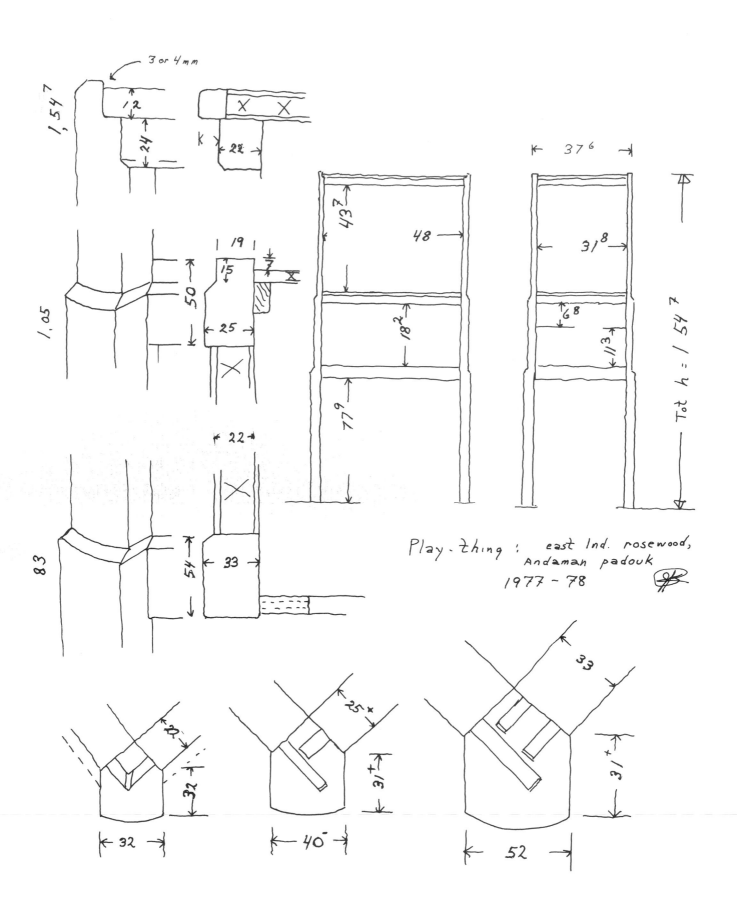

Play-thing: east Ind. rosewood,
Andaman padouk
1977 - 78

Accuracy

It seems to me there are mainly two kinds of accuracy. The first is the accuracy of the machine, of industry; an accuracy that allows for no deviation. A process is set up, the work is done, the result is certain—certain, that is, on the level one has chosen. The second kind of accuracy is what I'd like to call the accuracy of intent. In it there is a human element: our craftsman. He, too, achieves a desired result with a certain predictability, but in this case it is attained by his skill, which is a human thing, a reflection of the craftsman as he wants to be.

He is, let us say, a good craftsman who works efficiently, but with intentions all his own. There is a personal touch, style, and charm to what he does. Maybe one can manufacture and duplicate charm—I don't know, but I want to doubt that. At any rate, I imagine such a craftsman's accuracy is what we see in a piece with a personal air about it and nice details, a piece that is clean-cut, well done. It's an accuracy of *judgment*, which is more than just the accuracy of *method*. A craftsman who is to do this kind of work probably has to have a fairly independent nature, together with a sense of logic. He must be observant, and he must learn when to be relaxed and improvisational in his work and when to follow closely a very disciplined method, whether his own or someone else's.

One important qualification is being able to judge, for instance, when to use a machine and when not to. It's not always easy to know. We are told about a process: "It's

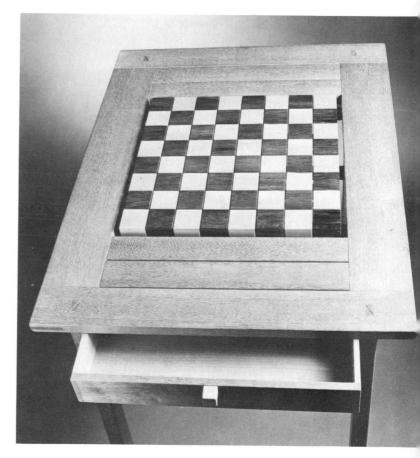

THIS PAGE AND FACING PAGE: *Chess table of doussie, playing surface of natural pearwood and Rio rosewood. Height 72cm, width 58cm, length about 76cm. Wax finish. 1978.*

quicker and easier to do by hand," someone says. "By the time you set up a machine I can do it by hand and do it better." This isn't always true. In schools, we have machinery much used by many people who don't care all that deeply about the condition of the machine for the next person who uses it. In general, these machines are badly tuned. Time is lost getting set up to use them.

With one's own small, neat machines, however, things should be different and better.

Steps along the way to the chess table: A seemingly simple piece, yet one that requires concentration and accuracy. It is worth the effort only if the choice of woods lends the proper aesthetic mood to the piece.

On such a machine one can do certain work both more quickly and more accurately than by hand. Take slip joints, for instance—something we saw very often. There may be four such joints in a doorframe or a frame-and-panel construction. "Do them by hand," someone says. "What kind of a craftsman are you when you cannot do them by hand?" All right, sawing such joints by hand is, of course, a test of skill. And I suppose if we are making a crude bed or a garden gate out of fir or pine or some other softwood, we can and probably should do these joints by hand, because it is a pleasing kind of work and we need the practice. But the same joint in a different situation—in a finely tuned piece using hard wood—is quite another matter.

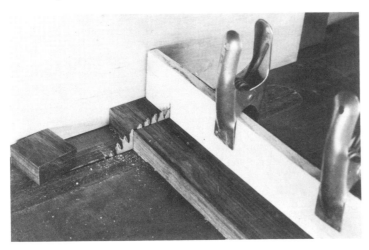

Sawing the squares: One surface and the two edges are first finished true.

Temporary frame around selected squares enables them to be flipped over (with the help of plywood piece) for drilling.

Wood—here Rio rosewood and pear—is sorted into light, medium, and dark. The aim is to have darker shades at the perimeter of the playing surface, the wood gradually lightening toward the center.

Sawing hardwood dowels: These must be very dry and of equal diameter. A drill to give a snug fit is ground with a spur.

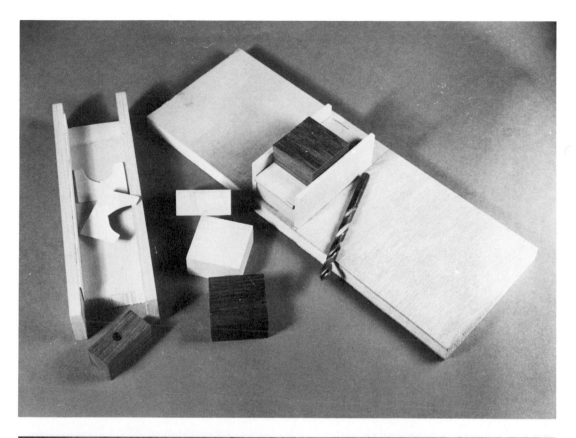

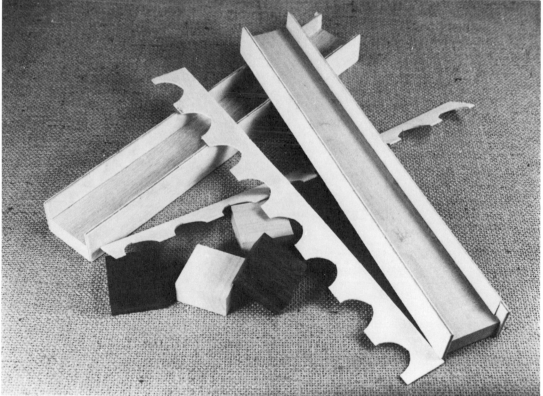

Preparations: Troughs and spacers (about 1/16″ thick) for gluing blocks in half and whole rows, and drill jig.

How many of us can saw one—not to say four—perfect joints by hand? Certainly not I.

Method of drilling: Blocks, upside down, are separated into corner pieces, the rest of each outside row (six squares), and the remaining inner area of thirty-six squares. Marks show the three configurations for holes.

Drilling: Each hole is drilled from edge to middle of square only. Going all the way through (on blocks with four holes) would lessen accuracy. The jig can be of plywood or chipboard, with rails giving a snug slip-fit for the squares. It must be centered with great care and clamped firmly in place (here on the horizontal mortiser). Any discrepancies are apt to be doubled when the blocks are assembled, and such errors, however small, grow along each row.

Nor do I think an improper fit—and it will be an improper fit that way, with hard wood, in a piece where tolerances are small and every little imperfection will show—can be excused in its defects by the fact that it was done by hand. When the table saw we work with is our own, and well kept, and we know that the right-angle guide is really at a right angle and the vertical fence is vertical and a smooth, even surface, then we can and should do the work on that machine. And I dare say it will be done *better and more quickly* this way than it will by hand.

At the same time, there is another aspect to the subject of accuracy: It is a matter of *attitude* as well as skill and logic. A lot of us harbor a kind of antagonism toward accuracy because we associate it with a dull mechanical process. And after all, as craftsmen—or at least as a certain kind of craftsmen—we want our work to show the skill of our eye and hands rather than the efficiency or exactness of a machine. As in so many other instances, it is again a matter of the pèrson being there in the finished product. This we want. Though we want it in different ways.

Before drilling for keeps, practice with trial squares. Turned face to face, they must still be in line.

Assembly: Beginning a row. The fourth dowel (connecting two halves) is glued into the last square of this group, and a half square with a larger hole, marked CL (see next photo), is slipped on when clamping. The piece D, also with a larger hole, is less than one-half a square in depth and serves as a stop when tapping the dowels home. The organized method is crucial; to forget the CL block or one of the spacers would be serious.

Clamping with the help of CL block.

The other half of the same row. Since no dowels protrude, it can be clamped without the protective CL block. The bottom of the trough must be short enough to allow this shorter half row to be clamped tightly.

We meet still another side of the matter when one of us says, "Anyone can be accurate. There's got to be more to it than that in *my* work!" Yes, there has to be more than that. Accuracy is not an end in itself. Although—and here's the crux—it *is* an important part of cabinetmaking, part of being a craftsman in this area of woodworking.

As it is, all too often we see examples of cabinetmaking—or at least furniture—where scooped-out slabs of wood (or band-sawed blocks) are put into costly and visually complex pieces, which to a few of us seem a sort of pretentious carpentry. As carpentry it may please some people; as cabinetmaking it leaves a fair craftsman wondering. . . . Coarse dimensions, bulging shapes, heavy-handed fits—*could* the person who made this have done better? *Can* he or she make a really nice drawer or a finely balanced joint? What is behind this insistent coarseness?

By its nature, cabinetmaking involves detailed work. One of the things that has happened is that the details have become fewer and more clumsy. The *scale* of some work has gone wrong and even within a given piece there's apt to be an imbalance. One reason could be that we are too absorbed in being creative, we're into things more important than details.

Another explanation might be that we do not have a feeling for details, or an eye for sensitivity. Or, even if we have a bit of these, we simply lack the skill needed to express ourselves in a sensitive way.

In certain quarters, a folksy attitude toward our craft prevails, making refinement rather suspect. At the same time, I believe a turning point is near; already some of the many new young woodworkers are aware that sensitivity and simplicity *do* go well together, and in a result that is more than just folksy. Because some of those going into crafts are doing so on the basis of an honest and broad outlook, their goal as craftsmen will not necessarily be an echo of what is now the idiom in this medium. I believe their aims will be modest, yet high—probably higher than ours are.

These people, most of whom are in it for the *experience*, have a notion of what sensitivity is about, even if some haven't as yet put it into practice. They see an added interest, challenge, and satisfaction in being able to determine their level of refinement and work on that level when the need arises. The importance of this awareness is already making itself felt. It will increase as some of us exhaust ourselves with the game of oversimplification.

Much of the frustration associated with exactness is a result of its being too rigidly taught. "You set up the machine like this: one-two-three. And you get this." I believe it is quite natural for some of us to rebel against that. Let me put it this way: Rigid methods/rigid results is one type of accuracy, whereas an exactness that includes flexibility gives another and richer result, and with it the craftsman's own kind of accuracy.

To better explain what I mean by *accuracy* or *exactness*, maybe I should go back to the very beginning, to a workshop with simple machines and fine tools, to a craftsman with patience and at least an inkling of true skill, who wants to express something personal in his work. We're apt to start sorting things out: the kind of work we want to do and the way we want to do it. In other words, what it is we want to say. And if we don't want simply to do as others have done, and do it quickly, then we begin more and more to rely on ourselves. Even if at first such reliance gets us into trouble, we still do want to rely on ourselves. We want to take learning and experience and information from others, yes, but always we have a need to interpret that and use it in our own way, because the work itself—and not only the result—is so important to us. Work here is more than hand and eye, or information and practice. It is these, *plus our own logic.*

Completing one row. Remember that last spacer!

After having glued eight rows: Preparing to assemble two rows together.

Two rows, with separating spacer, glued and clamped.

Probably somewhere early we begin to develop a logic of our own. Then, if we want to work neatly—or, rather, if we're the kind of person who *should* do neat and sensitive work—our logic develops along certain lines. We discover at an early stage that accuracy for us is *relative*, not *total*. One does a certain process—even on a machine—and the accuracy is apt to be less than complete; there are always small deviations. We must learn to see the importance or the unimportance of these, and to develop ways to handle them. How can you do it? Be yourself, observe, relax with your knowledge—and the rest will come.

Take, for example, something as simple as the curved, laminated frame of a door in which we are going to saw a slit for a slip joint. From the time we bandsaw the various

Next, gluing two rows plus two, and finally the four-row halves are joined to complete the surface of sixty-four squares.

layers of laminate to the time when we surface them, glue them, and then perhaps trim them by hand on one side, from the beginning of that process, there is the potential for a series of small—really very small—human deviations. Because it is a small workshop and we have neither the attitudes nor the machines of industry, there is an element of flexibility in everything we do, even by machine. So maybe one end of the laminated door frame is a thirty-second of an inch—less than one millimeter—thicker or thinner than the other. In fact, it probably is.

We are going to saw this slip joint; each slot must be equally wide to accept its other part. Yet there is a slight difference in thickness between the door parts. Rather than getting involved in trying to trim these down to one super-exact measurement, going from one piece to the other, taking a bit here and a trifle there, and maybe finally losing the minimum measurement we wanted, or cutting through a laminate, we simply choose a point at which to "aim" the accuracy we need. A primitive logic tells us that if we use only one side of each frame surface—the inside or the outside, depending—as our point of orientation and successively cut our slots with that side against the guide, the slots will all be the same width and depth. For our purposes it does not matter whether there will be a discrepancy of one thirty-second or so on the other, less important side, because we are going to work that part afterwards, either just before we glue the door together or after we have done so. The tenons, too, are done with the same logic: Depending on the occasion, we direct the accuracy we need to the part of our work where we need it most, then we adjust the other parts to this. The result is something neat and well done. With the desired exactness where we want it. And, I hope, with something I call a human element as well—

The frame-type tabletop: Since sidepieces are about 4½" wide, joint is made with tenon having a sliding heel.

Cross-pieces are mortised and tenoned, but not glued. Before gluing the frame, check to see that the opening for the playing surface is a square; the cross-pins can be trimmed narrower if necessary to insure this. A marked stick is a handy aid.

A second table, this one of Cuban mahogany. Notice the fineness of grain as compared to the doussie. Despite this, the wood might splinter when edge is planed to shape; hence the precautionary cuts with a knife.

Underside of doussie frame, glued: Cross-pieces are now positioned with help of spacers, clamped, and fixed in place with dowels let in about three-quarters of frame thickness.

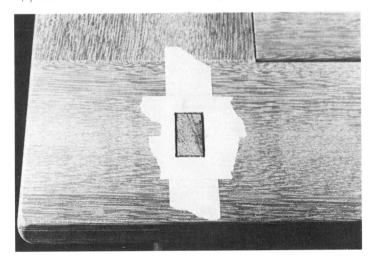

Leg with its tenon comes through frame and is later diagonally wedged. Tape prevents chipping out, a real danger with doussie. Note that the tenon has slightly beveled edges as an added precaution. When driven home, it will protrude a trifle; it is trimmed flush after gluing.

a live feeling combined with a neatness that cannot be explained by measurements alone. All along the way, for those who care, are situations where we can use this flexible knowledge, our kind of skill, on which so much depends.

The inability to humanize (or personalize) exactness and, with it, detail is, I suspect, one of the main reasons why some of us turn to exaggerated forms and impersonal techniques. Thus we avoid problems that require skill. But aren't we missing something? Aren't we perhaps too much afraid, too impatient?

Some problems are less difficult than we imagine them to be, and more interesting than we have been told. Industry can give us accuracy, schools can teach it. What they cannot—or will not—give us is the live feeling to go with it. That's where the real craftsman comes in.

LEFT: *Underside of finished table showing framework that supports the playing surface. It is screwed both to the table (unplugged holes) and to the squares. Cross-pieces of this support are aligned with the dowels that hold together the squares of the playing surface. At left is part of one drawer, the bottom of which extends only to the edge of the area comprising the playing surface. The block on the sidepiece serves as a stop for both drawers.*

Showcase Cabinets

It is a puzzle to me why there are not more interesting showcase cabinets around. Certainly, living habits don't exclude this type of furniture. We do accumulate objects that are pleasing to behold and deserve a nice home of their own. Perhaps too many people have a preconceived, discouraging notion about showcase cabinets. Cabinet-makers may share such prejudices. Or the technical problems of doing doors with thin wood parts and closely fitted glass may discourage cabinetmakers. I suspect this is so.

A way of getting past these problems is to use pretentious, special-effects glass and wild wood in all sorts of bubbly shapes. Interesting. Although we may be missing opportunities by not taking advantage of the effects that simple glass set in pleasing facets can create. Work with glass and wood, if it is to succeed, demands great accuracy, patience, and a way of conceiving and then doing a piece that is different from what some of us have been involved with. So let's talk a little about this.

Someone says, "Showcase cabinets do not use enough *wood!*" This can be true. One is prompted (by mirrors and such) to forget, or at least to neglect, that this is in fact to be a cabinet, not an aquarium or a bar.

Showcase cabinet of Tasmanian blackwood. Height 136cm, maximum width 78cm, depth about 25cm. Oil finished outside, polished inside. 1977.

At first, I, too, thought that showcases were not truly cabinets. Then, because I liked the function of such pieces—their being the home for things people have gathered and enjoy—I attempted to achieve some sort of balance between the wood and glass as related to the purpose of the piece. The real challenge of showcases is the pleasing interplay between you as craftsman and those who will use the showcase. You express something personal—your own version of a concept that is also a certain mood; at the same time, you make something for someone to use and enjoy in his or her way. Through usage this piece you have made will achieve further expressions.

Whatever mild interest I had in showcases from the outset has increased since then. It needn't always be so. Even a craftsman who tries to make such pieces with an open mind and a sense of the possibilities may come to the conclusion that it's not for him— simply because it is not the kind of work most compatible with his personality. Certainly, one of the things we should try to determine as craftsmen is the sort of work that is really for us. We need to know—the sooner the better. We are by our nature (the sum total of the traits we have or do not have) either finely tuned, meticulously inclined, or a bit of the opposite, the kind of people who do rough-cut, "unorganized" work. In the latter case this type of cabinet-making is a frustration. Probably after trying we will then leave it. For the rest of us, those who try and discover something interesting here, I think such work leads to further discoveries and an increased interest. Through one possibility you come to the next, and the next. That's the essential difference in our work between monotony or routine and this other thing, which really keeps it alive through the years. After all, I hope that some of us, in choosing our craft, are choosing a way to live and work and be happy doing it for a long, long time.

Generally speaking, there are four basic solutions to showcase cabinets. Each poses problems, and invites variations. There is the flat, one-piece door or two flat doors on the same plane. The second solution is a **V**-shaped single door or two doors set at an angle to form a **V.** Another will be one or two doors forming a convex curve. And last, a door or doors making a concave curve. There are advantages and disadvantages to each of these alternatives, and it is a personal matter which—if any—has a special appeal for a particular craftsman. The appeal will probably begin with something visual: the fact that one likes the way a **V** appears, the way light plays on its glass, the idea of related angles and proportions. Or maybe one of the curved doors is more inviting. Its softness, perhaps. At any rate, I believe the first thing that attracts us is visual, whether curved or flat or angled, glass and light as related to wood. After that, we must think in terms of the work entailed in any particular solution we like. We probably should try from the beginning to decide on something both possible and worth doing.

This matter of the worthwhile is partly one of experience. For a beginner it may be difficult to judge what is worth doing and what is not, because he does not know exactly how much effort these various projects require. Later on, he gets a better sense of this. Then he can relate more closely to the wood he has and the result he might achieve with the wood and constructions he knows enough about, and then arrive at some point where he either believes in the possibilities or he doesn't. If not, then it's best not to start.

Besides the idea with the various demands we might first conceive, there are in showcase cabinets an enormous number of details to be discovered; these we can play with, and use. Some, of course, are directly anchored to the construction we decide on. Others—such as the various sensitive shadings we can use in connection with the doors, or the top and bottom pieces, the thin strips with which we divide the glass—are largely decorative. The center of this kind of work is aesthetic, yes; but it is also the physical relation of wood to glass, the fits we need, and how these relate to the various steps of the work. There are perhaps more discipline and organized method in making showcase cabinets than in any other kind of cabinetry that I can now think of.

The sort and thickness of the glass is to be considered from the beginning. Once upon a time we had blown glass with a greenish or brownish tint; it was alive, the real thing. This is now almost impossible to get. The modern imitations of antique glass do not appeal to me, so when I cannot obtain blown glass I use ordinary clear glass, about three thirty-seconds of an inch [just under 3mm] thick. The average thickness of a door I make for a showcase cabinet, which is, say, sixteen by thirty inches or twenty-four by thirty inches, is usually slightly under three-quarters of an inch.

Simply put, flat doors are carefully chosen wood in pleasing proportions that belong to a well-balanced piece; they make a good first exercise. Curved doors are another and more involved matter. Usually one has to saw the laminates for the shaped parts and glue these up to the desired thickness on a mold. This is extra work, but it's worth it. I wouldn't try to make curved doors cut from a thick plank of solid wood. First, because it results in a lot of diagonal or wrong-way grain, which makes the cutting of rabbets or slots for glass difficult and weakens the joints; and second, since it is very hard to predict exactly the visible pattern of wood on the pieces thus sawn, we're apt to end up with an imbalance.

Once you have an idea for a cabinet and have considered the practical problems themselves, it is time to think also in terms of proportion. There are various possibilities with doors that may or may not be simple in their construction. By placing the horizontal and vertical parts of a door in certain relations to one another, we can change the proportion of a given shape or size *without changing the size itself*, and in so doing make a door seem wider or narrower; higher than it really is or not as high. There are options. Nor do the various parts of such a door need to be flush. There can be intentional yet slight differences in the thickness of some members, which will introduce little subtleties and divide up the elements to give us proportions within proportions. These divisions are not for the sake of complexity, but because they are pleasant and give us variation instead of a single impression. There is something for the eye to play with. And it adds challenge in the work, since such details are worthwhile only when neatly done.

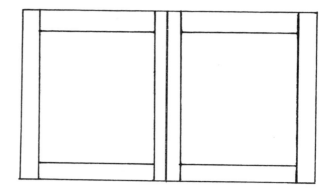

With curved doors it is best to have the curved parts themselves—that is, the top and bottom pieces of the door—extending out all the way. Thus the unbroken curve gives us a calm and complete sense of the shape of the cabinet; it is not "chopped off" by the vertical sides of the door. It is important to get this feeling of wholeness, to let the curve have its full intention. In such doors I find that having the sides, top, and bottom flush on the outside as well as on the inside results in a calmness; it gives the mood that goes best with the soft curved intention of the piece. One should try to accentuate this feeling in the details of the various other parts. Think soft. . . .

Considering proportions: Within the same outside measurements, variations are possible through the choice of the relationships of the parts. Grain patterns will add to (or detract from) these.

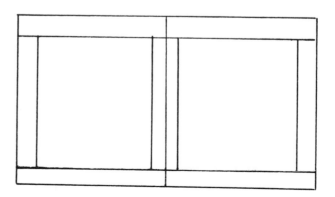

In its principal steps only, the work is apt to be as follows:

1) Concept of the piece, shape and size of door (or doors) related to whole.
2) If curves are part of the concept, mold for laminating. Saw and glue up laminates. Be generous with widths.
3) Vertical parts of door: Keep straight, true, and slightly thicker than laminated (horizontal) pieces.
4) Make slot and tenon joints as needed.
5) Dry-clamp, set up, then plan spacing of pins to take various widths of glass. Relate these to position of shelves and whole cabinet as you'd like it. A bit of composing . . . take your time!
6) Lay out and make template (or templates) for routing rabbet in curved parts of doors. *Do all this with care!* Have scribe-line along inside edge and stop-cuts chiseled at ends. Rout a little at a time.
7) Assemble doors. Mark for rabbet in outside pieces and groove (or rabbet) in middle ones. Double-check margins as related to machining. Make stop-cuts, scribe, and do all machine work, including bevel on inside of parts having groove. Before reassembling, plane the inward front edges on vertical door parts to a nicely rounded shape.
8) Assemble. See that rabbets or grooves meet as they should. Round edges along curved door fronts.
9) Make (shape) and fit vertical pins to hold separate pieces of glass. Cut them straight grain, and make lots of extras! Think about glass fit.
10) Glue up doors. Prepare everything, study setup. Dry-clamp first. (Neatness)
11) Clean all corners. Plane vertical parts of door to curve. Have plane iron razor sharp, fine set.
12) Do machinework for overlap fit of doors, angled to suit curve. Watch out!
13) Square doors. Check total width top and bottom *when in right curve*—make template or measuring stick—and proceed with work on cabinet case. (Lay out position of sides, how doors fit.)
14) Refit pins for glass, make rest of parts (to fit rabbets and pins) that hold glass in place, drill, countersink. Fit to doors using thickness pieces of wood (or glass itself).
15) Final fit of doors. Polish and finish all door parts (handles?). Remove doors. Complete case, finish, make stand if needed. Go through all details before hanging doors for keeps!

The above list, or something like it, would be one of those reminders I make for myself on a scrap of paper. Since the various procedures are closely interrelated, it will be difficult for me to give you an exactly parallel description to suit your project—we should be together doing the work. As I have been through it many times by now and am (almost) used to the zigzags, it is hard to foresee what your difficulties, if any, might be. For the time being, you'd just have to ask and, I'm sorry to say, even try to answer, your own questions.

Choose the wood carefully. Relate the graphics and the color to the intention of the piece as a whole. The choice of wood can make or break not only a cabinet that is all wood, but also a showcase cabinet. Don't fool yourself into thinking that with these cabinets the choice of wood is any less important than with others. Cut the various layers of laminate for the door with care, keeping them in a visual relationship to the cabinet shapes. I make them two and a half or three millimeters thick (roughly ⅛"); on a door about twenty millimeters thick there are seven or eight layers.

No matter how cautiously we work, there will be deviations along the way. Even at its best, our accuracy is not quite total. The laminated door parts will emerge nearly, but not exactly, of an even thickness throughout—and they are curved. The other pieces will need to be shaped (hollowed or rounded) later on to form the whole smooth curve of the doors. Before doing this, however, we must make rabbets and perhaps grooves in these vertical parts, and do so without going astray. Our objective, you see, is to have all the details coincide at the corners: We don't want to chisel and chip and scrape trying to fit glass to wood! To provide a working margin here I make the vertical parts of the door slightly thicker than the laminated parts. This gives me the chance to make small adjustments before machining, and to shape these pieces afterwards. Actually, the work is not as complicated as it may sound, though it is necessarily exacting. Once you get the idea, you will discover a certain consistent logic about planning layout and methods. From then on, you can work without further ac-

Layout of the curved doorframe and resulting support block for cutting slots in proper relation to ends.

Gluing laminated parts of doorframe.

The vertical members of the door are slightly thicker than the laminated curves; later, they will be planed to the curved parts. It's a detail one senses rather than actually sees.

Doorframe: Sawing the slot for tenon with the support piece held by spring clamp. This can also be done on a bandsaw. Cuts made successively will be parallel to the straight edge of the block.

cident—provided you achieve the right amount of concentration. Here, even more than in any other kind of cabinetwork, patience and care at every step are absolutely essential. If you are not set upon such an effort, perhaps it is better to avoid these cabinets altogether.

Having made the principal parts of our door—whatever the shape—and cut the various joints that are needed, we fit them together dry. Now comes the most critical part, namely, the rabbets in the top and bottom pieces. It is necessary to solve the problem of these rabbets before doing those in the sidepieces. If it is a curved door, we must make a very exact template of the curve with the various facets. But wait! To do this we have to know the locations of the various sections of glass: their widths and the thickness of the strips that will divide and hold them. This, in turn, should relate to the shape of the curve we have chosen, the size and proportion of the door. We must now back up a bit, to the point where we conceived the idea for this piece and, with it, the main parts, the relationship of the front to the rest of the cabinet. Right or wrong, some details could hardly have been more than a guess. Now, deciding on how the vertical strips, and behind them the shelves, will look, we do more than guess. The difference between right and wrong in spacing these various facets of glass is a matter of sensitivity, judgment, and experience. It's an elusive thing. And neither I nor anyone else can tell you when you've got it right. You, yourself, have to feel it.

Single curved door: Searching for the proper relationship of vertical pins between facets of glass. It must relate also to the shelves that will form horizontal lines. The door is slightly less curved along the midsection.

Facing page: *Cabinet with two doors. Spacing here related to the total curve, to the balance of each door, and to how the middle part, where the doors meet, suits the whole.*

To "get it right," even in relation to ourselves, we should experiment with various curves and spacings. I tend to make my curves more tense at the ends; that is, the door is slightly less curved along the middle and then tightens toward the outsides. And after some experiment I have concluded that the pins (the verticals dividing the glass) need to be closer together toward the outside of the door and farther apart at the middle. How much and how little depends upon the curve and, of course, how one feels about the shelves that are going to be in the cabinet. These make a horizontal division that is not obvious when you have only the door in front of you, so consider that there will be horizontal lines here and that they will "shorten" the door somewhat—in the case of a curved door, they will make it seem wider than it really is. I use thin strips of wood to simulate shelves and tape these onto the inside of the door between the horizontals. I can then move them up or down, observing how the "shelves" affect the door, until I arrive at something I believe will be fairly good. Someone says, "But I can use glass shelves, and then there will be no negative effect." That is not always true, although sometimes glass shelves do work very well. Usually this is because the door and the rest of the cabinet do not need definite horizontal lines to compensate for exaggerations or deficiencies of proportion. The cabinet is somehow intentionally or unintentionally *meant* to have glass shelves. In other cases, with a similar cabinet, shelves of glass may prove to be all wrong; one will discover this when one changes from glass to wood here. This is a matter of experience, of judging and observing, which also means experimenting.

Convex wall-hung showcase of Swedish maple. Height 88cm, width 56cm, maximum depth about 18cm. Oil finish outside, polish inside. 1976. This one has shelves also of maple.

136

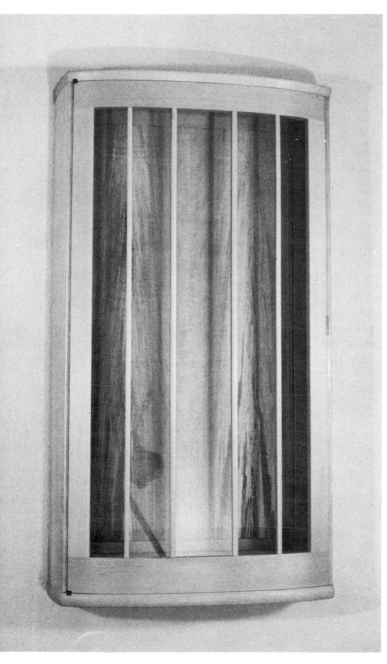

Without shelves, the same cabinet seems more elongated.

Glass shelves do make a difference.

Whether for glass or for wood shelves, I make two or three holes for shelf pegs or consoles at each of the levels that seem well placed, thus allowing for a certain amount of leeway. Another eye may find an even better variation on my choice. Let's decide on a spacing. And turn to thinking about making the faceted templates with which to rout the rabbets on the curved horizontals of our doors. Plan this so the depths of the rabbets will be equal at the various corners. (The measurement of this depth is from the inside of the door.) Do take time to get it as exact as possible, later our rabbets in the sidepieces (verticals) will be made to coincide with these, and early care will pay off then.

Usually I cut the rabbets about three-quarters of the depth (or thickness) of the door itself. In other words, there is rather little wood at certain parts (related to the curve and how we divide it) of the front edge. The glass is, as one might say, "up front" in the door, rather than being set back. I think this gives a sense of lightness; the door appears less thick and, therefore, less awkward. Besides, there is more room behind the glass for the fitted wood pieces to hold it in place.

Making one door only, we need a single template, which we shift from one surface of the clamp block to the other, being careful not to change its relationship to marks that indicate the positions of pins and rabbet ends.

We can do likewise with a pair of doors, or else make two identical templates, which we handily use without shifting them on the clamp block: The lower left-hand one is also the upper right-hand one, provided they are really accurate! All our planning is from the inside of the door. You will notice in the photos that the piece is clamped to the template so the router has access from what corresponds to the inside of the door part being worked.

Details of the door: Strips separating the pieces of flat glass are shaped to a curve intended to suit the softness of the cabinet front. If they were simply to follow the contour of the door, they would appear flat, being only about 10mm wide.

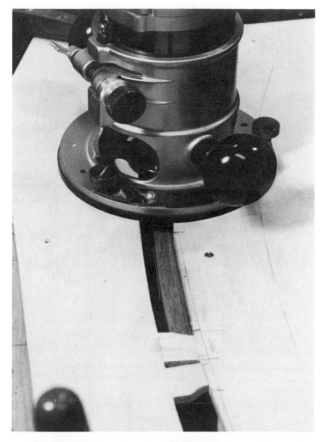

We concentrate our attention and accuracy where it really counts—to the way the glass will fit the door. If there are small differences in the thickness of the wood at the front edge of the rabbet—between the door front and the glass—it does not really matter all that much; a very slight variation here will bother no one. Granted, however, we do try to get each of our measurements as accurate as possible. Gradually, the relationship of details becomes clear in our mind; we coordinate the steps and methods that are important, and we master them. We learn how to plan: where to allow in our measurements, and how much.

Template for routing rabbets in curved parts of concave door. This one, with both its halves alike (it could be in two parts), is for a pair of doors. The widths of the glass pieces have been determined and carefully marked on the inside of the template to form straight edges. When routing, several small cuts are safer than one larger cut, which may cause chipping.

Seen from below: The door part clamped in place must be exactly in position. It has notches (stops) cut at each end of the area to be rabbeted.

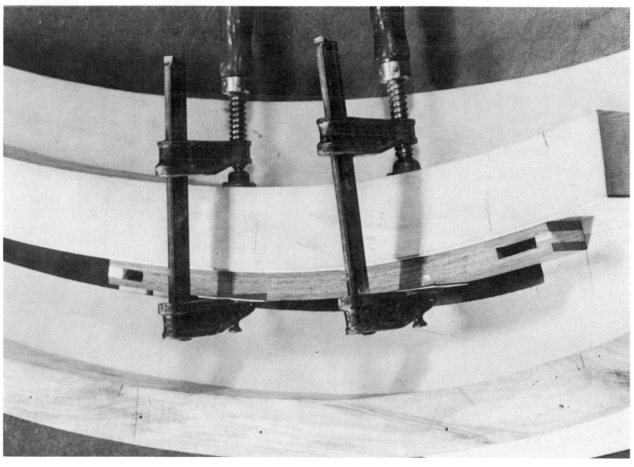

139

Scribe-line and stop-notch on vertical part of door to be rabbeted.

Where two doors come together, their parts are apt to be narrow. Here one can saw (or rout) a slot for the glass rather than making a rabbet, as is done elsewhere. From this slot, the frame is beveled slightly on the inside to afford a better view. All parts are trimmed as closely as possible before gluing-up.

In order to do the rabbets neatly, we must prepare the various parts by marking off exactly where each cut is to be made. Mark (while clamped up) the starting and stopping points of each cut, and chisel a notch there to prevent chipping out. Then, if the grain is at all difficult, it is safest to insure the lower edge of the cuts with a very fine scribe. We do the more complicated horizontal (shaped) pieces of the door first, then dry-clamp and mark accurately for the work on the sidepieces. Keep the margins as small as possible! With some doors, where one side (toward the middle of the cabinet) is narrow, I have a groove instead of a rabbet. This is machined to meet the adjoining rabbets precisely. And here again the accuracy needed is relative: an allowance on the inside thickness of this frame part helps us to arrive at a common depth from which to set exactly the table saw or router.

With the rabbets done, we can make the strips or pins that will separate the various panes of glass. From the beginning it is necessary to know the thickness of the glass we are to use. When we saw or rout the grooves to fit, there is one thing more to remember: The pieces of glass as they meet at these strips will be at a slight angle; the angle corresponds to the various facets making up the door in its curve. Each groove, therefore, needs to be a trifle wider than the thickness of the glass to allow for this slight angling. Do take this into account. It does not mean, however, that you should make the groove sloppy and allow too much for the thickness of the glass. With a poor fit, the glass is apt to rattle as a car passes outside.

Principal parts of one doorframe belonging to a pair of concave doors. This is the lower right-hand area.

Shaping vertical parts of door (after rabbets have been made).

Some of you may prefer to cut the various pieces of glass to fit. This isn't easy! Having tried, I now go to my favorite *glasmästare*, as we call glaziers, and have him do it for me. Before doing so I make a first assembly of the pins and the strips that are to hold these in place. Then, using scraps of thin plywood veneer, I cut slip-ins that correspond to the exact width of each pane of glass, all of which have a common length, namely the height of the door between rabbets. My *glasmästare* is very kind and patient; he cuts the glass extremely accurately. This, in turn, makes my work of final fitting much easier. If you plan to cut the glass yourself, try to do it as neatly as he does; it will pay off later on.

I have tried clumsily, with my photos, to show the various steps in fitting the glass and the wood parts that hold it in place. There are beveled strips at the sides of the door and shaped pieces in the rabbets, top and bottom, notched to fit the various pins between the sections of glass. Usually, when I make the laminated parts of the door, I make them wider at first than need be and then bandsaw two or three thin layers off the curved shapes. These I later use to secure the glass. With such pieces there is no slash grain, and they are neat and easy to work since they already have the shape of the door itself—I need only trim them to fit the rabbet and then notch them for the various strips themselves. I do not use screws here, but prefer brads. With these it is easy to remove the glass if need be by carefully prying up the hold-in pieces. First I drill holes in the strips the size of an easy fit for the brads. Then I place the glass in the door together with the various pieces of fitted wood to hold the glass. With a slightly smaller drill, now a very tight fit for the brad, I drill through the various parts at a slight inward angle, making my hole deep enough for the whole brad. I countersink ever so slightly for the head itself. The brads are small and hardly noticeable, so they do not bother us as we view the cabinet. I take it for granted that we have tapped and then set them without leaving any marks on the wood.

Steps in fitting parts to hold glass in place: Drilling for brads with help of wood spacers, countersinking for brad head, and so on.

142

Yes, all this is a bit of work, one slow, careful step at a time, the outcome always at stake. Not everyone should try to do such work. This I say to myself even as I do it....

Before polishing and setting in the glass for keeps, I carefully fit the door with its hinges to the cabinet. To allow for the fact that it will sag a trifle from the weight of the glass, I make the door fit a bit tightly upward. Then I polish the door and the various strips that will hold the glass in place. If there is to be a handle, I fasten this to the door. In other words, I finish everything possible before I put in the (clean) glass and hang the door.

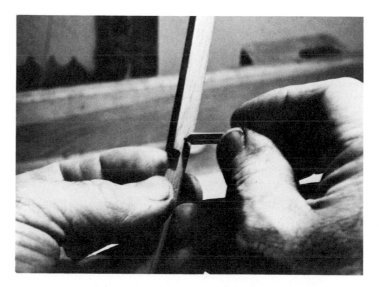

Door complete with glass in place.

143

Basic parts of convex door, inside view: The two grooved pins at the middle are a trifle wider than the ones at the outsides.

FACING PAGE: *Showcase with single door set in a mild* **V**. *Swedish maple. Height 86cm, width about 46cm, depth 19cm. Oil finish. 1965.*

*Beginning the **V**-shaped door for the Swedish maple cabinet. One-piece blank gives basic door shape without complex joint.*

Two outer parts, mitered, form the rabbet. Note the thin pieces of cardboard used to raise each of these slightly while drilling for stop-nails (for gluing). When they are let down and glued, the parts will fit even more tightly.

The principal parts of the **V**-shaped door. Shading around spline tenon is a slight chamfer to aid clean glue-up. The fit must be (and stay) aligned if bevels on frame parts are to meet.

The outer (thicker) part of the sidepiece is separate. One edge is finished before the piece is glued with the aid of small, ⅛″ dowel guides.

Trying to describe showcase cabinets, I find myself talking mostly about a door or doors and the process of making and fitting same. It seems a rather dull and one-note description. Actually, a showcase cabinet is much more than a door or doors, or a glass front with a few objects showing through. Still, the door is usually the most difficult part. I feel, therefore, that special attention to it and its problems is justified. Because, when we can make a door on the level of our intentions for the rest of the cabinet, I believe the chances of success are very good indeed.

Our showcase cabinet is more than a glassed door or two. We should be aware of this rather early, so that when we sketch or draw or otherwise plan the piece with its important front, we think of it in relation to the whole: the degree of detail and refinement, the proportions, the amount of the back that will be exposed, how the shelves will affect the proportions as well as how they will cast their shadows upon the backpiece itself.

The door is glued in only one direction at a time; the other half is merely set in place dry. Special blocks for gluing have coarse sandpaper against door surface.

FACING PAGE:
*Making and fitting the middle pin: A hardwood blank (darker) is glued on as a stiffener. The **V** angle is hand-planed exactly along the 7/16"-wide strip. Then a bevel is machined almost to the point where the slots are cut for the glass, after which the glued-on stiffener is removed. The glass is pushed into the slots and let down to rest in the rabbets at the top, sides, and bottom, where wood strips hold it in place.*

148

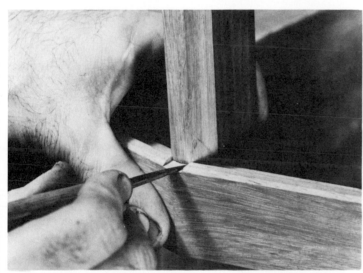

150

Another point: Usually included in our idea of such a piece is the way it will be used—on a wall at a certain practical height, or perhaps with a stand that should be a pleasing part of it. Try to get a clear impression of these possibilities. When looking at the work during the various stages, imagine (or simulate) the final way the piece will want to rest. Come as near as you can to reality. This ability to achieve a well-balanced whole is dependent on observation (which becomes experience), and it is natural at first to be uncertain. When thinking of a stand, we may be tempted to imagine curves, shapes—not *just* a stand. All right, let your fancy go, but then allow for some other considerations: How will the stand serve its purpose, which is to support the case at the most pleasing height (with the doors *open* as well as closed)? How will the stand harmonize with the case? Harmony includes lines, and also volume; a stand has "weight," just as the case does. In reminding you of simplicity and harmony, I don't intend to be an inhibiting influence; certainly a person with a mind for fantasy and taste can combine flare and harmony skillfully.

A variation of the **V** *door: Two smaller doors (about 60cm) in wall-hung cabinet of lemonwood. Total height 64cm, width 71cm, maximum depth 18cm. Oil finish. 1966.*

A last practical note: In showcases that have curves, the sides are apt to be set at an angle, which complicates the joints needed in a strong and well-made stand. I usually make these angled joints with spline tenons done neatly on the horizontal mortiser (that too-often overlooked machine!). Take time to lay out properly, get all the angles correct and fits sung. Dry-clamp, and then study the stand with the case together. . . . Return, and look again. When you decide to glue up, have everything you need, including the specially fitted blocks that go with getting such pieces together.

I hope and believe some craftsmen will go into this kind of work, discovering possibilities and satisfactions of their own. My attempts are limited; the illustrations here are meant only as a beginning. There is a great deal more to be done than I have even imagined.

For those who try this path and then decide to abandon it, here's a consolation: One can learn something about oneself along the way.

"Those People"

It bothers some of us to think that we will, if we do our very best and then decide to sell our work, be making rather expensive pieces. I have heard craftsmen say, waving a hand roughly upward, "I just cannot see making things for those people. They could buy your shop and house, too, along with the piece, but still want to bargain about an honest bit of workmanship."

I share that feeling, but I will not be bound by it. Traveling reminds me again that there is little or no connection between wealth and that thing called good taste. Nor does money make someone a better person, or a worse person either. What it probably amounts to, for some of us at least, is that we are doing honest work, our best, with feeling in it, and we hope to meet people who will appreciate and want it. Some poor people with whom we get along very well will understand and say that they are sorry, but. . . . Another person, of modest means perhaps, might ask to pay a bit at a time, and something tells us to trust him or her. Wealthy people come and ask the wrong questions and we feel so uneasy that some of us just do not care to let them have the piece. But there are also some with money and taste and a simple warmth that gets through our "those-people" filter; we enjoy telling them about our work, they listen—there is contact, a kind of understanding.

Nothing else matters, really. It is all about people. The best we can do, if we need to protect our own feelings or ethics or whatever, is to sort things out in such a way that we associate with just people, regardless of what they have or do not have; the only qualification being that they are *the kind of people who do not make us unhappy at our work or about our work*—that is vital. Then, if we are modest and live accordingly, we will be fair about what we ask. And these other people, whoever they are, will be fair in what they give.

Or is that being impractical again?

Following pages: *Cabinet of natural (unsteamed) pearwood. The stand is Italian walnut, drawers of Lebanon cedar with Rio rosewood fronts. Height about 154cm, width 44cm, depth 19cm. Outside finished with oil-based wax, inside polished. 1978.*

Conclusion

Returning from a long journey, I find myself more hopeful than before. It has been predicted that the best work of the next few decades will be done by amateurs, craftsmen working not primarily for a public, but for the sake of values they believe in and the work they love. Now this is not so much a prediction as it is an awareness of what has already begun. Even if some of these craftsmen accept the fact of selling, it is no longer their primary motivation. The sell part is a consequence of conditions, and acceptable only when people appreciate the work and the reasons for it being what it is. So a new pattern is emerging. There is a quiet warmth. People are finding reassurance in simple contact and ways of working that fit their outlook on life. The trend is irreversible. We will get an interesting, fair counterweight to the contrived and overly competitive in our craft, which has been all too prevalent for much too long. A balance is certainly needed, not only because the quiet craftsman has not been getting his due, but also because there is—there certainly must be—a potential public that has been sorely neglected. People living and working quietly somewhere off to the side, out of the mainstream of crafts shows and promotion, are doing good, honest work that is interesting for exactly the reason that it is good and honest, has a warmth and a directness of its own. These qualities might at first puzzle a public trained to eccentricities and recognizable techniques, which is a pity. It is missing something.

There is a lack of communication between some craftsmen and a public that would, no doubt, be interested in their work—if it was told about the work in the way the craftsmen and the work deserve. Craftsmen are not all verbal about all this, but they do want others to see what they have made, and talk about it. There is a natural need to share, but simply, unpretentiously. This is best done if we others know at least a little about what they, the craftsmen, are doing: how and why, in the important sense, the feel and the meaning of their work. We need to grasp the content of an intimate kind of workmanship. This would be a new and deeper experience for many of us. And it would, though we do not seem to want to realize this, make economic sense as well. All of which is difficult for the public to grasp.

We have not been given a chance to contact these people, much less a basis for understanding their work. What some of us would like to see now is a bit of help from people writing about crafts, critiquing and presenting work in wood. We could wish for the kind of competence and perception and stimulating interest we get, for instance, from serious music criticism. As a rule it does more than name the music that was played and who played it. It is not enough to interview someone who says he does work that will last 300 years, or that he wishes he had been born a tree, or to report a person doing sculptured pieces as a superb craftsman. There are enough sculptors who are good artists and technicians but definitely not superb craftsmen. We could change the emphasis from names, styles, and techniques to values that include aesthetics and the integrity of workmanship.

Sometimes it is tempting to imagine a quarterly publication with such an objective purpose. And seminars, where fewer of the usual "big-name" craftsmen would be present and more educators, critics, and would-be critics, those doing craft books, and certainly people from all walks of life who simply want to sit in. Workshops attract mostly craftsmen; conferences tend to be stuffy; crafts fairs and large shows are often distracting in the overambitiousness of their scope. We might try something else.

If I were to express one further wish, it would be that, under whatever circumstances, people who look at craft and sometimes want it should come close enough; they should look for the person in the object, because that is what the new generation of crafts will be about: personal attitudes, personal touches in the work, where simplicity will be a sign, not of weakness, but of strength. The trend is toward a rediscovery of the content of work, leading to forms and expressions that are enriched by the intimacy of method, the presence of someone doing his best. The things these new craftsmen will offer you will have more than just a visual appeal, more than decorative or investment value. Honest purpose, clean lines, the traces of tools skillfully used, these make up objects that enrich us in a person-to-person way at a time when so much of our lives is spent in anonymity, in hurried commercialism and bureaucratic trivia. We need something, even a single object, to remind us that there is another, more generous side to life. Things made with love and received with understanding—that is what might yet bring it all together.

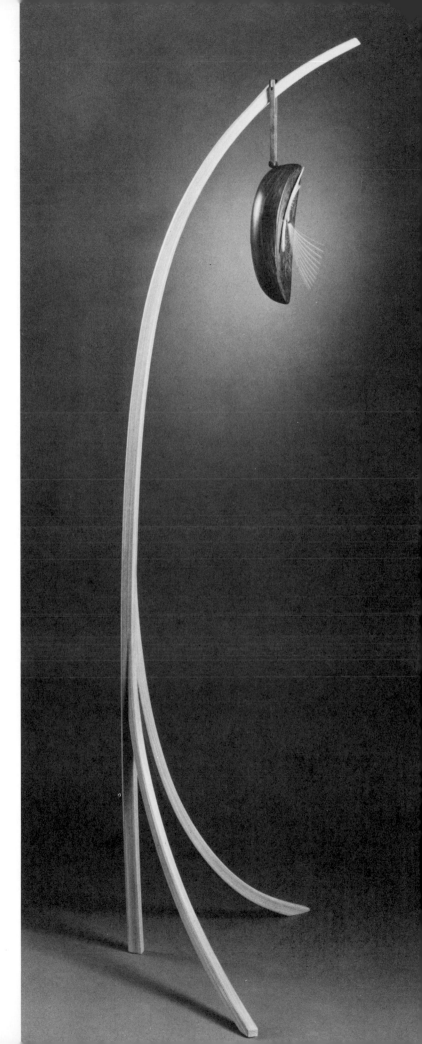

Cocobolo clock on stand of laminated elm. Hour and second hands only. Height of stand is about 160cm. Wax finish. 1978.

OPPOSITE:
*The Rio rosewood cabinet. Drawers
are of natural pearwood.*

Index

Italics indicate illustrations.